For a Girl

Mary-Rose MacColl is the author of five novels, including *In Falling Snow* and *Swimming Home*, as well as a non-fiction book, *The Birth Wars*.

For a Girl

Mary-Rose MacColl

ALLEN&UNWIN

SYDNEY • MELBOURNE • AUCKLAND • LONDON

This is a true story. Some names and details have been changed to protect privacy.

First published in 2017

Copyright © Mary-Rose MacColl 2017

Allen & Unwin
83 Alexander Street
Crows Nest NSW 2065
Australia
Phone: (61 2) 8425 0100
Email: info@allenandunwin.com
Web: www.allenandunwin.com

Cataloguing-in-Publication details are available
from the National Library of Australia
www.trove.nla.gov.au

ISBN 978 1 76029 523 3

Set in 12/18.5 pt Fairfield Light by Bookhouse, Sydney
Printed and bound in Australia by Griffin Press

10 9 8 7 6 5 4 3

MIX
Paper from
responsible sources
FSC® C009448
www.fsc.org

The paper in this book is FSC® certified.
FSC® promotes environmentally responsible,
socially beneficial and economically viable
management of the world's forests.

I HAVE A PHOTOGRAPH OF a girl of ten. She is standing by the convent pool she swam in every Saturday of that summer, in togs with a striped border I don't remember owning. She is in the left of the frame and the background is an overexposed blur of water and the shapes of children. Her face is brightly white except for the freckles scattered over her nose and cheeks. Her hair is stuck to her forehead. She is grinning, saying to you, the observer, 'I am here.'

My body remembers

WHEN OUR SON OTIS WAS tiny we lived in the gentle university neighbourhood of St Lucia in Brisbane, in a seventies town-house with soaring ceilings and a balcony that overlooked a bushland park. A butcherbird perched on our railing and sang most mornings, mournful or joyful, depending more on the listener than the bird. Two frogmouths, mother and baby, spent their days in the tree outside Otis's bedroom in his first months in the world. Frogmouths are nightjars, related to owls, wise. I thought they could keep him safe.

On weekends we'd put Otis in his all-terrain stroller and walk along Hawken Drive to the university for gelati from the Pizza Caffe above the Schonell Theatre. One Sunday, when Otis was not quite two, we met up with my husband

David's sister Lisa who was off to London to live. We'd had our gelati and Otis had coated his shirt in chocolate and mango. Now he was running around on the grass.

When it was time to go home, I called Otis and then, when he didn't come, chased after him. I picked him up under the arms, his little legs still running through air in the way of busy toddlers. I sat him in his stroller and rolled up his shirt, the gelati now melted and cold on his tummy. I strapped him into his stroller and he screamed.

At first I thought he was objecting to the restraint and I started to be stern. I wanted Lisa, who'd just finished a PhD in psych, to think well of me, to see me as a mother who set limits. Then I saw I had pinched his belly in the stroller clip. I undid the strap and picked him up and held him. He cried for half an hour. It left a claret-coloured bruise that lasted two weeks.

When we arrived home, I went upstairs to the bathroom and shut myself in. My right leg was shaking, the long thigh muscle in painful spasm. I slumped against the door to keep myself upright. The shaking spread to my pelvis, belly, left leg. I fell to the floor. Noises came from me, a low moan, a louder cry. My teeth were chattering, making the cries come out in an odd staccato. If it weren't so terrifying, it might have been funny.

David knocked on the bathroom door to ask what was wrong. I had been quiet on the way home. I told him to leave me alone. I screamed at him to leave me alone.

After some time—I don't know how long—I came out of the bathroom. I had no idea what had happened. The next day, I felt as if I'd run a marathon. Every muscle in my body ached.

In the weeks that followed, I told myself I'd been upset because I hurt my little boy. Any mother would feel bad about hurting her child. I told David. I told friends. You know what it's like being a mother? I said. They didn't quite understand, I could tell. They had felt bad for accidentally hurting their children but not like this.

⌒

When Otis came into my life, I understood abundance. His birth: I have never felt so powerful and exposed and exultant. David was there, my friend Louise. Afterwards I was buoyed by a community of friends and relatives who shared in our joy of new life; even people we hardly knew looked upon us with joy in their own eyes. Otis was perfect and he made me feel perfect. Nothing of the drudgery of the weeks and months that followed could extinguish that light of joy, and whatever I have faced since cannot touch it. In Otis's first months in the world there was enough joy for a lifetime.

At the hospital where I gave birth, I heard one midwife call to another that the woman in Room 2, me, was an elderly primip. Elderly is used to describe any woman over thirty-five—the obstetricians who make up these terms being noted for their sensitivity—and primip is short for primipara, from the Latin *primus*, first, and *para*, to bring forth. To those midwives, to most people I knew, I was a forty-one-year-old woman giving birth for the first time.

Gail Sher says that writers, by doubt, enter the way of writing. I wouldn't have described myself as elderly at forty-one, and I wasn't primiparous when Otis was about to be born. I had given birth twenty-three years before, to a baby I named Ruth. No one knew. Baby Ruth was a secret because of other secrets, much darker than the birth of an unplanned child in those disco days of the 1980s. When I pinched Otis in the stroller clip, baby Ruth came back, demanding to be grieved, and with her came the secrets I had kept for so long.

I am by nature a private person. Secrets are different from privacy. They are things you are forced to keep to yourself, by family, friends, by your own shame. Secrets like these come to the surface one day and demand an airing. If you don't allow them air, you will not go on. They will drag you back down with them. You will die, slowly or quickly.

If you allow them the air, bring them up into the light, they float away.

PART I

Wandering

Happy families are all alike

WE ALWAYS HAD CHRISTMAS WITH my mother's family when I was growing up: her three brothers, their wives and twenty or so kids, along with Mum's mother, my nana. The menu was chicken and potato salad, followed by watermelon. There were devilled eggs at Tom and Mary's, brandy flames on the plum pudding at Tony and Jill's, and no pudding sixpences at ours because Mum worried about the choking hazard.

I famously danced on the table when I was two, my uncle Tom encouraging me into a frenzy, a whirling dervish, everyone in fits of laughter until, inevitably, I collapsed in tears in a plate of watermelon.

I was full of beans, Mum said. I look ridiculous in photo-graphs taken in my early years. Mum cut my thick hair straight across at the front in a blunt fringe, forming a right angle on each side. My chubby cheeks pushed my eyes closer together, and Mum told me, many years later, that Nana believed there was something wrong with me mentally—based on the fringe rather than the whirling dervish incident, although the whirling dervish probably didn't help.

My oldest cousin, Marg, used to visit our house with Nana. Marg would have been ten when I was two. When they arrived one day, I was in the sandpit wearing nothing but a nappy, using the wedding silver for digging tools. Even Marg knew, she said, when she told me the story years later, that something wasn't quite right, that the silver wasn't for digging. I was the third baby; the fourth was on the way. The next day, Nana came back with Marg, bringing with them Nana's cleaner. No one remarked on this, Marg said. The cleaner sorted out the house while us kids gobbled down the cakes Nana brought from the Shingle Inn cake shop in the city. And then they left.

⌐⌐

Mum used to drive us around in the car on Sundays after Mass and we'd get lost. There was a man at Mass, Joe, who had cerebral palsy, and before we went on the drives Mum would always stop and talk to him. Others, including me, gave Joe a wide berth—spit came out when he talked and he had trouble with words. Mum would seek him out. She'd struggle to understand him, but she'd stay there until they'd had a reasonable conversation. Then she'd wish him well and tell him she'd see him next week.

On the drives, I think Mum only pretended we were lost. We had a big old Austin called Granny that had belonged to Nana and the back door would sometimes swing open around corners. My two big brothers, Ian and Andrew—one of whom would always reach across and pull the door shut when it flew open and frightened me—were much better at finding the way home than I was. We lived in a spec-built weatherboard house in Chapel Hill and all the roads were dirt, so Granny would fill up with road dust and Mum would lead us in a song she composed called 'I Wonder How the Dust Gets In'.

When I was four, my brothers and I were taken away to a children's home north of Brisbane. I think Mum's younger brother, our uncle Tony, the doctor, drove us there. He may have found the home. It also might have been Tony who told us Mum needed to have a rest.

Soon after I arrived at the home I was stared at by a doctor who had a moustache. I'd been told to strip off to my green cottontail underpants to be weighed and he was staring at me. Did they provide us with clothes? I think they did, even the green cottontails. I didn't like being in cottontails in front of the doctor. I might have bitten him. I still had the fringe so it's possible that, like Nana, he thought I was mentally unhinged. I don't recall a punishment.

My older brother Andrew, closest to me in age and a beautiful child, told a care worker to shut up when she said something nasty to me—I wet the bed and it may have been about that. She told him if he said things like that she'd have to wash his mouth out with soap. He told her to shut up again and she washed his mouth out with soap.

My younger brother Lachlan, not yet two, was in the babies' section at the home, divided from us by a high wire fence. When I went to the fence to talk to him, he threw himself on the ground and screamed. I think he wanted to get out. One of the workers on his side of the fence shooed me away. Mum came to visit us on the Saturday with Nana, who brought chicken. I don't remember anything they said. They left and we were there for what felt like a long time. It was two weeks, one of my brothers said later.

Tolstoy said all happy families are alike. Jeanette Winterson's mother asked why be happy when you can be normal. Our family didn't have the wherewithal for even the semblance of normal. Dad worked from around four in the afternoon until one in the morning. He was a journalist on the sub-editing desk at *The Courier-Mail*, so he helped to create the newspaper each night. Mostly Mum was on her own with us kids.

In the mornings, we had to be extra quiet because Dad finished work so late and needed to sleep. I would lie in bed and tell myself stories or get up and make funny faces in the mirror. If we did make too much noise, and this happened frequently, Dad would yell from the bedroom. If we were really noisy, and this happened frequently too, he would stomp out and yell at us in person.

Our house was a mess. We drew all over the walls in crayon. We didn't pick up after ourselves. At school, we never had those pre-peeled oranges other kids had. We might have benefited from Supernanny but there was no Supernanny in those days and I know for a fact I would have hated her. I can't even watch the show as an adult without becoming annoyed.

We were more Addams Family than Brady Bunch—not like the Wadleys, the even larger Catholic family contemporary to ours: Nana's friends Sir Douglas and Lady Vera; their two boys John and Peter, who grew up with Mum; John's wife Denise, who'd worked as a journalist with Mum before either of them married; and a stack of kids we went to school with. If we were whirling-dervish-wedding-silver odd, the Wadleys were Denise's-column-in-*The-Courier-Mail*-Fig-Tree-Pocket-family-fun perfect. We wore our damage openly because we didn't have a choice. Perhaps if I'd seen their back rooms I'd have discovered that other families, maybe even the Wadleys, were damaged too.

While we weren't normal, I wouldn't have said we were unhappy—not us kids, anyway. Mum was a kindly presence in our lives and enormous fun when she was feeling bright. Dad wasn't kindly really, but he wasn't present much either. I remember noticing a difference when I first visited other children's houses. One family at Indooroopilly had twins the same age as me, and their father ran around chasing them with an axe. When he caught them he hog-tied them in the backyard. As I say, it's possible every family has its damaged places, but the father meant well, I'm fairly sure. I do recall a sense of alarm as he held the axe above his head and screamed at his son in a way my father probably wouldn't have screamed at Andrew. He said he was an Indian.

The first thing I learned at school is that being full of beans is not helpful in a classroom with forty other children, at least as far as teachers are concerned. If someone had thought to explain it to me that way—I'm sorry, dear, but no one can keep forty children still for six hours straight—instead of saying I was the problem, for wriggling, for talking, for being bored, I think I might have hated school less.

As a child, I was routinely mistaken for one of four boys rather than the only girl in our family. I watched the wrestling on the television wearing underpants and a singlet so that I could act it out, and I wanted to be a range of superheroes, all male. My gender identity, although that wasn't what I would have called it, was to do with clothes—my brothers' pants and t-shirts, and that haircut favoured by my mother (who at some stage bought a bowl for the purpose, which at least smoothed the right angles off)—but also what I came to like. Mum and Dad gave me a doll for Christmas one year, and I gave it to the girl up the street. My brothers were my first playmates. I played their games. They treated me as one of them. I felt like one of them.

I was the smallest in my class, and also the youngest. There was nothing I liked about school, not the routine, certainly not the uniform—a dress—and not the rules. I was often labelled attention-seeking, as a criticism rather than a compliment. I was still so small by year three that one day, when I'd been down to visit Lachlan, who was still in preschool, I was mistaken for a preschool child from a distance as I headed back up to the big school. I quickly ran away from the teacher, who was beckoning me back to preschool. For weeks afterwards, I expected she'd come up to the big school to get me and take me back to prep for being too small.

By then, I'd discovered that when you're small the best way to get noticed is to do things you're not supposed to do. I became quite good at it. I liked being noticed. I don't know if this is more or less considered normal for children. I don't know if I had some deficit in my sense of self that made me feel not quite good enough or if all children feel that way. I've often wondered, given what came later. Was I marked from birth? Was there some flaw in me that made me more likely to falter on the road to adulthood? And if there was, exactly what was it? I did have an absolute belief that grown-ups were good, perhaps because in my childhood most of them had been.

Mum normally dropped the two big boys at the train for their school in the city and then took me to the convent before dropping Lachlan at the preschool. One day, I was sick—not terribly sick, a little fever—but Mum said I could stay home with her. I watched as the preschool teacher peeled Lachlan one finger at a time from Mum. After we left, she bought me an ice-cream and took me for a drive and I didn't have to find the way home. I remember the winter sun coming in through the windscreen on the way out to the farmlands of Brookfield, having Mum all to myself, and then waking with melted ice-cream all over my shirt when she stopped the car in our driveway, being mad that I'd fallen asleep and wasted some of the day we had together.

The midday movie was *The Old Man and the Sea*. The old man was losing his fish, and I couldn't stop crying, loud gut-wrenching sobs. Mum, who very much wanted to see Anthony Quinn in the role of Hemingway's great character, was perplexed about what to do. Finally she turned down the sound and we watched it silently. There wasn't any dialogue and without the sad music, my cheeriness returned. My uncle Tony suggested, when Mum told him later what she'd done, that she could have turned down the brightness as well and we could have watched the black screen together. When I swallowed Jesus, Mary and Joseph from our nativity scene a few years before it had been Tony who'd said, when Mum rang him in a panic for medical advice, that it would be better if she rang the priest.

⌒

My brothers and I developed an outstanding collection of comics and other kids would visit us just to read them. As we grew older, all our friends hung around our house. Mum made toasted sandwiches in the old style, using a frypan and a ton of butter, and accepted a broad range of behaviours. One of Andrew's friends wrote me after we'd met up in middle age to say he'd had cause to reflect on his life and the handful of people who'd been kind. My mother was first among them, he said.

Mum had married Dad when they were both journalists at *The Courier-Mail*. It was the society wedding of the season, Margy told me. Mum had already finished her BA and a Diploma in Journalism at the university. Dad had dropped out. Mum was paid less than Dad, and quit work late in her pregnancy with Ian and never went back.

I have two photographs of my mother. The first was taken when she was small, perhaps a year old, and it is in a plain wooden frame on my wall. She is sitting on a table against a nondescript background dressed in nothing but a nappy. Black curls surround her face. Her hands are busy.

Her eyes welcome the world. She is smiling, not at the photographer, but at something else she can see beyond the frame.

In the second photograph, which is in our family's album, she is wearing her university graduation gown. She is still smiling but her smile is smaller, manufactured. Her eyes would not welcome the world. She has learned something. She is wiser but would not trust you, not really.

I look at these two photographs of my mother and wish I could have changed whatever it was that took her smile from her. I have hazarded a guess, as many adult daughters have had to do, because that generation never told their secrets. Loyal to whoever was requiring her silence, Mum never in her lifetime, nor in her journals left for me, spoke of what had knocked her from happiness to unhappiness. But something had.

That was the second part of what Tolstoy said. Happy families might be all the same, but unhappy families are all unhappy in their own way.

I have worried you'll think poorly of me on a number of counts—you have plenty to choose from—but I hope from the outset you will try to understand my mother. Your other mother has been so different from mine, different also from the mother I am to Otis.

I can see the questions your other mother might ask about my mother. What was my mother doing when she should have been banning her children from drawing on walls? Why was she letting us read nothing but comics? Why didn't she stop what happened from happening?

She's your grandmother, my mother, and I want you to think well of her. I love her very much. As for keeping what happened from happening, I don't know what my mother could have done to protect me. I only know she would have done it if she could.

Byron

TODAY WHEN I SWAM THE bay a perfect rainbow made an arc from Mount Warning to the pine trees where my swim finishes. The sea was as bouncy as Tigger and I took the rainbow for a good omen. During the day I had the sensation of gentle rocking as if I were still of the sea. Late in the afternoon another perfect rainbow, or the same one, ran across the sky in front of our veranda. You could argue that those rainbows were put there for me.

This week we are staying in a cottage on a farm above Byron Bay in northern New South Wales. We stay here every Easter. David goes to Bluesfest, and Otis and I visit the beach early in the morning before the crowds arrive. Sometimes we find remnants of the night before: bottles, a fire pit, occasionally sleeping people who do not wake up even when the sun is high in the sky.

When I can, I swim from The Pass at one end of the scallop bay where there's a sheltered cove and a shaded beach. While I'm in the water, Otis, now five, builds in the sand with David or makes face paint out of the different-coloured rocks. The first time we brought him here, that year I pinched him in the stroller clip, he ran around and around in circles at full pelt, so taken by the marvel that is a beach.

I go into the water, dodge the dive boats and surfers to get out beyond the break, and swim an easy kilometre, with the tide, to the surf club. Sometimes there are big waves to negotiate. Sometimes it is calm and I go out through the rocks and around the point where we see dolphins and occasionally whales from the lookout. After the swim, I walk back to The Pass and we eat toast with avocado and Vegemite and boiled eggs for breakfast.

Swimming in the sea has much to teach me. Last year I saw a shark. It's possible I channelled the shark, having been obsessed with them ever since I started sea swimming twenty years ago. My shark may have started its day at Lennox Head, coming when I started my shark thoughts for that day.

Otis, who has a book about sea creatures, used to try to help me with my fear. Sharks don't really like the taste of humans, he told me. They only take one bite because they think you might be a seal. He appraised me carefully. 'Maybe don't wear those black togs,' he said. Leaning in conspirat-orially, he added, 'And definitely do not swim breaststroke.'

David read a *Guardian* article suggesting you make your-self vertical in the water, as a shark won't be able to get a purchase on you to bite. If you've been attacked, you should make yourself vertical then punch the shark when it comes back around.

I could imagine treading water despite a leg wound bleeding me out from that big artery, but the idea of punching a shark was beyond me, even in my wildest imagination. And I am a novelist, so my imagination should be wilder than average.

The morning I saw the shark, I had swum out on my own, before the gaggle of swimmers who walk along the beach together at eight each morning. The water was clear. I'd seen two turtles when I swam over the rocks at Clarkes Beach. A voice in my head, some preconscious visual response unit in my brain, said, 'You're going to see a shark and it will be all right.' Before I could get the word No! that was forming in my head out through my mouth, there was the shark, below me and to the right, bigger than me, the biggest creature I have ever seen in the water.

I swam for shore as fast as I could, without kicking so as not to arouse interest. I ran back to The Pass without stopping. I wanted to live.

I wanted to live.

This holiday, we are becoming a family again. We are not a normal family but I think we are starting to be happy.

In your other mother's first letter to me, written when you were around six years of age, she said, 'I want to tell you about your beautiful daughter Ruth, whom we call Miranda.'

I wonder how long she worked on that sentence, for it is wise and generous and cannot have come easily.

Aye, Dugald

WHEN I FIRST VISITED SCOTLAND in my late twenties, I expected to be welcomed home. I knew from my mother, who was enamoured of my father's French–Scottish ancestry, that the MacColls ran the place. My father was the eighth Dugald in his line. When we learned the 'Skye Boat Song' at school, I knew my own ancestors had played a part in this rich history. One of the Dugalds had been in the boat guarding Bonnie Prince Charlie as he fled the invading English to the Isle of Skye, my mother said (although if you google it, Dugald the guard doesn't come up straightaway). The MacColls were poets whose names and verses rolled off their Highland tongues.

Imagine my shock to learn not only that the MacColls weren't running the place but that no one I met in Scotland was named MacColl. We didn't even have a Tartan in the coffee table book at the B&B we stayed in. But how beautiful was my country anyway, with its mountains and lakes and majesty; how much I felt I'd come home after all. Walter Scott said it right: 'Breathes there the man with soul so dead, Who never to himself hath said, This is my own, my native land!'

My father was very clever, but he didn't like us kids much, a truth it took me some years to accept. It's possible it wasn't personal—he disliked most people—and I do think he may have disliked me less than he disliked my brothers, although it's equally possible I've imagined that.

On his weekends off, Dad did the garden in the afternoon and then drank beer and smoked cigarettes while he listened to Johnny Cash: 'Don't Think Twice, It's All Right' and 'I Walk the Line', or even 'The Long Black Veil'. His humour, which my mother later described as 'adult', was often hard to understand. He would ask, 'How old are you?' Seven, you'd say. 'Do you want to live to be eight?' Yes. 'Then shut up.' At one time I think I may have believed you could be killed for talking, which was not an easy cross to bear when you liked to talk more than just about anything.

Dad was oddly against the Cuisenaire rod system used to teach mathematics when I started school, in which colour-coded bars of different lengths are used to demon-strate addition and subtraction. He went to see my teacher. 'She knows that black plus white is tan, but if I ask her to add seven plus one, she looks at me blankly.' The teacher nodded sagely. 'All in good time,' she said, 'all in good time.' My maths never improved.

I'd sometimes make myself stay awake until Dad came home from work at midnight or one in the morning and we'd talk. I don't remember much about the conversations, just that he noticed me and spoke to me. One night when I was nine I cooked him an Irish stew while I waited. I knew he liked the mixed herbs so I put in the whole jar—not right at the start, but bit by bit until I saw there was none left. It wasn't a failure of Cuisenaire to help me understand the amount required, just an inability to recognise that a little of a good thing doesn't mean a lot will be better. When Dad arrived home, he sat down and ate the stew and said it was delicious. He put so much pepper in his potato—Deb powdered mash—that it was charcoal grey on his plate, so perhaps a bottle of mixed herbs was about right.

Dad set high standards. Once, when we were looking at a report card where I'd done well, an average of six on a seven-point scale, he focused on the subject I'd been rated a five in. I asked, 'What would you do if I got straight sevens?' There was no hesitation in his reply: 'I'd tell you to get eights.'

If people visited our house, Dad would go into his bedroom to hide until they left. It was a great joke among us kids—Dad has his paper bag over his head today so he doesn't have to be anybody. If he was caught before he got away to the bedroom, he was good company and people always liked him. That was the odd thing. Once, when a visitor made it through the front door before Dad could reach the bedroom, he went out into the backyard instead. He managed to get my attention through a window. I had to sneak out with his beer and cigarettes.

He told me once that his own father had done the same, shunned visitors, hidden if someone came to the house. My grandfather was André Dugald—André from his French mother—the older of two sons by seven years. The younger son, René Michel, was preferred by their father, who was Dugald Sutherland, DSM, an art critic and keeper of the Tate Gallery in London in the early twentieth century. The Dugald before Dugald Sutherland was a Scottish Presbyterian minister at the fire and brimstone end. I don't know the Dugalds who preceded the reverend, but feel certain we're never more than six Dugalds of separation from Bonnie Prince Charlie.

Before he'd turned twenty, my grandfather had served as an officer in the Argyll and Sutherland Highlanders in World War I. After the war, he worked in Malaya before emigrating to Australia on the toss of a coin (America was heads). In his thirties, he married my grandmother and refused any financial or other help his family offered. His letters home—DSM's personal papers are held in the University of Glasgow Library—are full of self-recrimination. In one, he mentions a sketch DSM has sent him and makes the point that he knows nothing about art and will not make a fool of himself by pretending to know anything. This kind of self-deprecation might have been standard with the Dugalds, but what surprised me about my grandfather's letters was the sweet love he expressed for his son, my father. He says he wants to provide the best for his son—Pip, they call him—says he can't believe how bright Pip is, what a marvellous boy he is turning out to be.

The letters were written before my grandfather went away to his second war. He enlisted in the Australian Army in World War II, lying about his age as he was over thirty-nine by then. I think he might have gone to earn money. He served in Egypt and came back suffering from what I assume was post-traumatic stress disorder. He was in a special hospital for some months. There are no letters to England from then on.

Among my father's personal papers there are only a few photographs. My favourite is one of him at two or three years of age in shorts and a woollen coat—a gorgeous, cuddly child by any account. He's in the left of the frame, running along a sandy shore full-pelt. Although the shot is low-contrast grey, you can see the energy in his limbs, an energy I never saw in the man. On the other side of the shot is his father, crouched down, arms open, waiting to receive his son in a hug. It is so full of love, this photograph, on both sides.

In another photograph, my father looks about ten. He's dressed for a party in a pirate suit. His father would still have been away at war. He has a cutlass at his side, an authentic hat, a vest and ragged pants. I don't know who took the photograph, my grandmother most likely, but the look on my father's face is one of quiet disdain. He is saying, 'I hate this stupid suit, I hate you taking a photograph, I hate my life.'

In the university library in Glasgow, there is a letter from my father, written when he was eleven, to his grandfather, DSM. He says he bought a cricket ball from a boy in his class and his dog Tim is highly excited. That afternoon, he has been across the road where a new house is being built to play tag with his friends. He is trying to make model aeroplanes but he is not much good at it.

Reading the letter made me realise my father was once a boy with a boy's sensibility. Like all of us, he was a product of his circumstances. His father's absences, first at war and after the war, suffering the effects, were not something he signed up for. Neither was his role among the Dugalds. I don't intend to excuse him—there is probably no excuse for disliking your children—but he didn't sign up for the life he had. None of us do.

My father was not flawless. He was a talented writer from a young age. He came to drink. He drank a lot. In brown swimming trunks, he looked more vulnerable than you could ever imagine a full-grown man might look. As I say, I never really understood him, although he was once the second most important person in my life. I would certainly wish him well in his next.

Heroes

I READ SUPERHERO COMICS ALMOST exclusively when I was growing up. I liked the orphans best. There was Dick Grayson, whose parents had been shot by robbers, taken in as Bruce Wayne's ward to become Batman's Robin. My favourite was Kal-El, jettisoned as a baby from the exploding planet Krypton, landing on Earth to be adopted by the childless Ma and Pa Kent, growing up to be Superman. I still sleep the way Superman flies, left arm straight up and under the pillow, left leg straight, right arm and leg bent. A physiotherapist told me it's bad for my back.

Growing up on comics, I believed that goodness would prevail, even once I started interacting with the education system, where goodness is sometimes well disguised. In comics, there is never a chance that villains will win. When Superman turns up, he triumphs unless there's Kryptonite involved, and even in his weakness, Superman is strong.

With a head full of superheroes, I began early to fashion heroes for myself from the grown-ups in my life. When I was four, there was our next-door neighbour John, a sales rep for Edgell. John used to get us promotional material to play with: huge cut-out stands of children eating peas and cardboard boxes with pictures on them.

One afternoon, I was sitting on the back steps. I was sobbing. John saw me from his side veranda and came down to see what the matter was.

'My brothers are loved more than me,' I told John between sobs. 'Ian because he is the oldest, Andrew because he is the tough one and Lachlan because he's the youngest.'

I expected John would share my devastation, offer commiseration. But he only smiled kindly and said, 'But, sweetie, you're the only girl. They love you for that.'

It was like the sun coming out from behind a cloud, this realisation. I'm the only girl. Of course I'm special. Toddling upstairs with this new knowledge, feeling like I'd won some race.

In year seven at Our Lady of the Rosary, when I was eleven, I found a new hero. After Mass one morning, the brothers stopped to talk with my class. I met Brother Bob, a tall slight man in his twenties with lamb-chop sidelevers.

He smiled at me. I made a joke about his black suit. I made him laugh.

I became a regular attendee at morning Mass. My mother couldn't believe it when I asked her to drop me to school early. After Mass, Brother Bob would stop and talk to me— not about anything in particular, certainly nothing religious, but we'd talk and then he and the other brothers would go back to their college. He might have wondered what to do about this funny little girl who started turning up at Mass every morning. Perhaps he liked the attention. Perhaps I annoyed him.

I decided to play a joke. The twelve brothers from Xavier College always came to Mass in their minibus. I spent a whole weekend making a big gold 'Just Married' sign. On the Monday morning, the morning Brother Bob always came to Mass, I tied it to the back of the brothers' bus while they were in church. I thought Brother Bob would find this funny. He didn't much like some of the older brothers with their strict rules. He'd know who put the sign on their bus and he'd think this was a good joke. I didn't go to Mass that morning. I hid down at the school and watched them drive off with my sign on the back of their bus.

I don't know how long it took them to discover the sign, how long it was on the back of their bus. But someone told Mother de Montfort, the school principal.

Mother de Montfort sat down outside the year seven classroom with me. She was given to shows of temper.

I remember another time I'd done something and she threatened to cane me. But she didn't threaten to cane me on this occasion. She was quiet, worried, tender even, and it scared me. She spoke kindly. First she wanted to know who'd put me up to it.

I was insulted she didn't think me clever enough to come up with the idea by myself. 'No one, Mother,' I said indignantly.

'You can't do that,' she said. 'We have to respect the brothers. You just can't do things like that. It leads to sin.'

Many things led to sin, although Mother de Montfort was never willing to go into detail. We were left to guess, and I had no idea. I knew it was something to do with the intensity of my feelings. I felt discovered, not for what I'd done, painting the sign, but for the feelings I had for Brother Bob. I never went back to morning Mass. I never saw Brother Bob again.

When I finished primary school, I started at All Hallows' School, which had educated three generations of women in my family before me. Nana was well known to the nuns at All Hallows'. She grew up on a farm outside Stanthorpe and she'd boarded at All Hallows'. Her best friend at the school later became a nun there. The nun was still teaching at All Hallows' when I arrived.

When Nana married my grandfather, they set up his medical practice in Fortitude Valley, just down the road from All Hallows'. My grandfather was a doctor for many of the nuns. Mum told me they used to go to lunch at my grandparents' house. They ate in a separate room because you weren't allowed to see nuns eat.

The nuns from the school who knew Nana sought me out after I started at All Hallows'. They pulled me into bony cuddles and looked at me as if I were a sweet they wanted to eat. One of them called me down to her music room, made me sing notes to the piano—Nana, an accomplished violinist, was said to have perfect pitch—before dismissing me as a poor tuneless girl. 'You haven't inherited the music, eh?' she said and let out a little laugh.

For a long time, I felt lost at All Hallows'. There were no boys, and boys were what I was used to. Eventually I found a group of girls to join but, looking back now, it wasn't a nice group to be in. We became the troublemaking group, which didn't worry me so much, but someone—mostly me it seemed at the time—was always shut out. They would call me names and I would be alone at lunchtimes because no other group of girls would want a troublemaking girl like me as one of their number. I was not used to shutting people out and being shut out. It was not something my brothers and their friends had ever done. I used to hide under a tree by the sports field until the bell rang so that no one would know I was alone.

Outside of school, I hung around with a group of neighbourhood boys. I still looked and acted like a boy. Over time, more girls joined the group, and some of the boys and girls started 'going with' one another, for anything from two days to two months. Francine was going with Craig. They kissed—pashing off, we called it. I was going with Craig for a few days after Francine dumped him for Pat, but when Pat and Francine broke off, Craig was there to comfort Francine and they were going with one another again. I wasn't one of the popular girls. I was too much like the boys for that. I sometimes wished I could be more like Francine, but mostly I liked being me.

In year nine, there was one girl in my home class at All Hallows' who was part of the group of girls I'd landed in but who was nicer to me than the others. Wendy had five brothers and was a tomboy like me. She was mostly my friend even when the others in the group weren't. We did things together in the holidays, went to a YMCA camp. I went and stayed at her house on the coast once.

Wendy and I both liked our maths teacher, Sister Maureen, who had an Irish accent. I remember a weekend detention when we had to help Sister Maureen clean up some part of the school. We set off the fire alarms by overloading the incinerator with cardboard boxes. Sister Maureen thought this funny, smiled with sparkling eyes as we heard the sirens of the fire engines coming from Kemp Place, kept smiling until the principal joined us, when she tried to look stern, her feet in sensible shoes pointing outwards, her hands demurely clasped in front of her.

Sister Maureen was one of three teachers at All Hallows' who became heroes. The second was my English teacher in year eight, Mrs Thomson, who saw how much I enjoyed writing creatively and inspired me to think about the importance of the words I used and the stories I told. The third was my science teacher in year nine, Sister Dominic Mary, who was strict and smart. She seemed old to me then but she was probably in her twenties. I remember she asked me to stay back after class one day. 'Your other teachers tell me you muck up, but you don't muck up in my class. Why?' I don't know, Sister, I told her. 'Are you scared of me?' No, Sister. 'You could do better,' she said finally. 'You ought to think about that.' Science was the only subject I did well in that year.

There is no doubt I was headed for trouble at All Hallows'. When I did something wrong—disrupted classes with what I believed were clever jokes, pressed the emergency stop button in the elevator, set off the fire alarms—the nuns who taught me would talk to one of the old nuns, who would ring Nana so she could tell Mum. This must have been excruciating for Mum. Nana was a wonderfully engaged grandmother but a domineering mother. Mum must have dreaded every Saturday visit from Nana while I was at the school.

My report cards were full of those stock-in-trade comments: 'attention-seeking', 'disruptive in class', 'talkative'.

I was troublesome enough to frustrate my year ten class teacher so much she locked me in a cupboard so that my evil spirits wouldn't get out and infect the other girls. I don't remember what I did that led her to put me in a cupboard. I remember her tears as she closed the door, which frightened me more than her stern voice. Her chin quivered with the upset. She died some years later of breast cancer. When I think of her I wish I'd been kinder.

I left All Hallows' when the nun who put me in the cupboard—who was also the deputy principal—called my mother in for a meeting and told her they would not have a place for me to repeat year ten.

'Well, we don't need a place,' my mother replied. 'We're going to another school.'

On the way to the car after the meeting my mother was indignant on my behalf, and I still love her for it. It couldn't have been easy, for she must have known that I deserved to be thrown out, and she must have known that come Saturday she would have to answer to Nana for my leaving All Hallows' suddenly. She never once mentioned this as a difficulty—that her wayward daughter had been thrown out of the school of her forebears, the school all my cousins and at least one branch of Wadleys were excelling at—and it is only now that I can see what it might have been like for her.

Your other mother's letter are full of such love for you. I wonder if you have read them. When you have troubles at school, she

describes you as spirited, blames the teacher who doesn't under-
stand you. She must know how biased this appears. I think
she doesn't care, in much the same way as I don't care when
someone accuses Otis of doing something or being something
they find uncomfortable.

I think you have a right to this: a mother who will overlook
your faults, who will stare in the face of your grown-up accusers
and tell them, Yes, yes, you are right, but this is my child and
I have only love. *It's what my mother did for me.*

Our first heroes surely are our parents. I know mine were.
Even when I failed in school, I wished I'd done better to
please my father. I loved nothing more than when my jokes
made Mum smile. We spend our childhoods adoring our
parents even when they fail us. And all parents fail. I'm sure
of that now that I am one. We use the marvellous energy of
adolescence to push away, as we must. We come to adulthood
and, if we're big enough as people by then, we begin to see
our parents as the real, flawed, beautiful people they are.

But for children like me, who sought heroes other than
their parents, adolescence is a time of particular risk.

My teacher and her husband

SHE WAS MY CLASS TEACHER in my second year ten, and I hated her. I hated most teachers automatically but I hated her in particular. I hated her odd clothes—pressed white slacks and colourful floral blouses, with flat shoes. She was like someone trying but not quite managing to achieve a particular look.

I hated her hair parted almost at her ear. I hated her strictness, which was forced. Everything about her was forced, fake. When I think of her now, I think of those Russian matryoshka dolls, the first doll hiding another with a different face, and another and another until, finally, the tiniest doll, and then nothing. She was not authentic as a strict, tough teacher. She talked about the army. Her husband was in the army. I gave her a nickname. I called her Bomber.

The school I'll call Saint Catherine's was a small, local Catholic school where Religion was called Christian Living. It had a strict principal who glared at me in my interview and said, 'Now tell me something: how is it that a girl can get a grade of one in every subject but English?'

'I like English,' I said.

'Indeed,' she said. 'But if you can do well in English, you can do well in everything. So are you lazy or are you trouble as well?'

'A bit of both, Sister,' I said.

'I thought as much. Well, you have a chance to start again here. Do you want to start again?'

'Yes, Sister,' I said, because Mum had told me to say Yes, Sister, to everything, but also because at that moment I truly wanted to start again. I was sick of being the child known only for trouble. I wanted to be something else too, although I had no idea exactly what.

I changed in my first months at Saint Catherine's. I found I was actually quite clever; not as clever as my older brothers, but clever enough to find some subjects interesting. I had a mix of friends, some of whom were tough, naughty, most of whom were good girls. I was still talkative, difficult at times. But I worked at my studies and made friends. The buildings at Saint Catherine's were modern. There were fewer places to get lost in. The fees were nothing like those at All Hallows'.

The girls came from families that didn't have wealth, like mine. I thought I might be happy there.

In the second half of my first year at Saint Catherine's, my teacher became one of my heroes. It probably happened gradually, but I remember the moment our relationship began to change. We were on a school Christian Living camp. There had been singing. I played my guitar. The priest had talked to us about love and sharing. There were not so many rules I could get in trouble for breaking. Everyone was more free and loose than at school. We were soft and ready to forgive one another. My teacher was less strict and it made her more real.

In the evening on the second day, I was putting out cups for tea and my teacher was helping me. As people came up, she suggested cups for them. 'Here comes Jessica,' she said. 'She needs a cup that will hug her, don't you think?' I couldn't believe she had a sense of humour. It was like another Russian doll opened up and here, finally, was something real. She was funny. I was giggling with her as we made the tea. We were more like two friends than a teacher and her student.

On the last day of the camp, she gave me a book of Charlie Brown cartoons. She marked with an asterisk the ones she thought relevant to me. I don't remember any of them now, just that I pored over them for weeks to try to work out what they meant.

In the months that followed our camp, my teacher would talk to me after school. Sometimes I would wait for her for half an hour, an hour. When she came out on her way to the car, I leaned down and pretended to be working on my bike so she wouldn't know I'd been waiting for her. We talked about the things I worried about, the way life should be. She was a mentor to me, supportive and concerned for my welfare. She was interested in me. I told her things I'd never told anyone else. I worked harder at school. I did well.

My teacher was unpopular; even the well-behaved girls disliked her. There was that lack of authenticity about her in class and kids are quick to pick up anything false. But outside, after school, she listened to me, counselled me. I didn't really talk to my mother about problems and while I was closer to my father than my three brothers were, it was more like I was in a temperate zone in his heart while they were in the tundra. We had no family friends I could turn to. There was my uncle and aunt Tony and Jill, who I was close to when I was younger, but we hardly saw them in my teenage years. We lived in our world and there were few grown-ups. I didn't tell my friends I was talking to Bomber after school. They would have made fun of me.

One Saturday towards the end of the year, I visited my teacher's house to do something for the school with a friend. I can't remember what we were doing, something for the end-of-year party. I was thrilled to be going to her house, to have been asked, although I didn't tell my other friends about it. I would have been embarrassed to admit I was going to her place. The friend I was with was one of five beautiful daughters with a strict father who protected them with curfews and threats. She didn't like Bomber much either but came to be with me.

We met my teacher's husband. He was working in the garden, wearing Speedos and a t-shirt. He stood up when we arrived, arms out from his body, legs apart. He had short dark brown hair parted neatly on one side. He was so thin it made his head look too large. He smiled and told us my teacher was inside, called after us to have fun. When we were leaving later, he was washing the car. He turned the hose towards us, just missing us, and laughed. His eyes lit up when he laughed.

In my year ten Christmas holidays, my teacher asked me over to her house one Sunday for lunch, on my own this time. Over the next few months, we became friends. In the next year, my year eleven, I went there after school, on weekends. I started calling my teacher and her husband by their first names.

At first it felt odd but soon I became used to my teacher being my friend. My teacher and her husband ate foods I'd never heard of, chicken casseroles with real wine in them. They drank wine too and so did I when I was with them. I felt grown-up. They had people to visit, people from the army.

Their house smelled good, of clean washing. They used fabric softener in the washing machine, I learned, and it made things smell nice. They gave me attention, much more attention than I got at home. Their spare bed, when I slept over, had clean sheets that smelled of the fabric softener. I loved being there.

When I visited my teacher and her husband, I was on my own. My other friends from school didn't know and my teacher and her husband suggested it would be best not to tell them. I readily agreed. My friends would have thought less of me if they knew I was friends with a teacher like Bomber. A couple of times another teacher asked me if I was spending time with them outside school. I lied and said no. She didn't believe me, continued to question me. When I told my teacher and her husband about it, they said I must never tell anyone we were friends. They said the other teacher, the one who asked me the questions, was out to get my teacher, that she was jealous. They told me things about other teachers in the school too, explained that many of the other teachers were jealous of my teacher because she was a very good teacher. I believed them.

Initially, I think Mum thought my teacher and her husband were a good influence. They sat in our lounge and drank tea, while Dad hid in his bedroom. They were responsible, sensible people, and I was a wayward girl. I had been asked to leave All Hallows'. I needed guidance. Maybe they would give me that guidance. Later, Mum saw how much

I looked to them for counsel, and I'm sure it worried her. But by then, I was absolutely convinced that they were good people and my parents were fools. My teacher's husband had told me as much. My mother couldn't tell me what to do and she knew it. She did say something about me spending time with them, but I ignored her; I knew better.

By the end of the first term of year eleven, I was spending most of my spare time with my teacher and her husband. When we were out, people sometimes thought they were my parents. I liked it when this happened. I wished they were my parents. I thought they were better than my parents. My teacher's husband knew so much about the world. He gave me advice about what bad people were like, who to watch out for. He was so sure of himself, so confident in knowing right from wrong. As for my teacher, she continued to listen to me and provide advice. I believed everything she told me. I thought they were the best people I'd ever met. I felt lucky. I loved going to their house with its fabric softener smell.

Sometimes we went for trips in their car. My teacher's husband had an interest in cars and drove fast. We went to Toowoomba with another of his friends from the army and my teacher's husband drove at over a hundred miles an hour. His friend followed but couldn't keep up. On the way home, they took me to a restaurant for lunch. It was the second time in my life I'd been to a restaurant. The first was with my friend Wendy's family. That was a Chinese restaurant.

This was a buffet restaurant in Toowoomba. I had never seen so much food.

There were stories my teacher's husband told about himself. Once, he told me, he pulled a pistol on the driver of a car full of young men who yelled something suggestive at my teacher. He forced the driver off the road, got out, put the gun to the man's temple and said, 'Did you want to say something?'

He also told me that army officers would never wear their uniforms in a magistrate's court because they might embarrass the magistrate. Everyone had to stand for the magistrate, who had a certain rank in relation to the Queen, but the magistrate's rank was not a commission like an army officer had. Technically, my teacher's husband said, the magistrate would have to stand for an army officer. I believed everything he said.

My teacher's husband had strong views, black or white, and when he changed, the change was total. Black became white. He eschewed formal education until he enrolled at university and then it was the best thing a person could do. He owned expensive Italian sports cars until he had a serious accident, not his fault, and then he bought a Holden and lost interest in cars. He moved to music, which he'd had no interest in before. He bought a stereo that took up most of the lounge room and cost thousands of dollars. My teacher and I listened to John Denver. Her husband listened to *The*

Firebird Suite and the theme from *Apocalypse Now*. He bought records that tested his speakers and listened to those.

He was never disingenuous. A thing was black or white and sometimes it changed from one to the other. The change was sincere and it was absolute. He described himself as superhuman and worked hard to make it true. He was fit, did well at study once he started. He had been badly injured in his mid-twenties when a fire extinguisher he was disarming blew up. The doctors wanted to amputate his arm but he said no. He rehabilitated himself and regained almost full use.

To the girl I was, my teacher's husband was larger than life. I believed he was as powerful as he made himself out to be, but even so he wasn't a hero. We had nothing in common.

I am reminded just now of *Women Who Run with the Wolves* by Clarissa Pinkola Estés and the story of the ugly duckling who approaches all manner of creature before she finds her pack. I had no idea who my people were.

⌒

My teacher's husband had a temper. I don't know how much was his nature and how much was his experience in Vietnam; he turned twenty-one there and while he seldom spoke of his experiences, a youth spent in a war is no youth. One lunchtime he lost his temper with me. I disagreed with something he said and I remained firm in my disagreement as he became annoyed. I don't remember the subject. I'm sure I provoked him. I think I wanted to see what would happen.

His face drained of colour except for a vein in the middle of his forehead that pulsed slowly. He set his eyes on me and walked over to the chair where I was sitting. Without saying a word, he picked me up and tossed me over his shoulder, just like that. I called out to him to stop, half laughing with the shock of it. Then I struggled to get away but found I could not. He carried me into the bathroom and put me into the tub and turned on the cold shower tap and said in a quiet voice, 'There, that will cool you down, you bitch.' He left me there.

My teacher came and helped me out of the bath. She didn't say anything to him. My clothes were wet and clung to my body and I felt self-conscious. I also felt the aftermath of fear, catching my breath. And I felt ashamed. I had never made anyone this angry. It was shocking to me. My teacher's husband was so strong, superhumanly strong. He was a grown-up, in charge. If he was this angry, it must be my fault.

Byron tsunami

OTIS AND I WERE ON the beach this morning when the police came along in their truck. In the company of a child building castles with drips of wet sand—an enormously satisfying activity—it is hard to muster up any energy for negative emotions. Even sharks can seem benign.

The Byron Bay police are as relaxed as people who make sand-drip castles. They stopped on the beach and then a slow-talking metallic voice came through the loudspeakers on either side of the truck. *'There is a tsunami scheduled for eleven o'clock somewhere along the east coast of Australia. It's your decision to remain on the beach. We're just giving the warning because that's our job.'* I wondered at the use of the word 'scheduled'.

On the Gold Coast, I learned later, they closed the beaches, but this was Byron Bay, where individual freedom was highly valued.

I thought of Indonesia, as many people did. I heard conversations on the way to the car.

'The sea sucks out first.'

'Well, when it does, we'll go home for lunch.'

'It's a ripper and apparently we're deadset in its path.'

'Wicked!'

'Which board d'ya reckon?'

Otis told me it was probably called a tsunami because sometimes the army comes. That sounds about right, I said. We headed for higher ground and the farm. The cows saw no danger they could tell us about.

I have a writing table here at the farm, simple pine boards on tube-steel legs on the veranda of our cottage. The table overlooks a hillside at the bottom of which is a deep dam that runs into a creek where we found dragonflies such as I haven't seen since my childhood. Today the cows are on the opposite hillside. You can watch cows for a long time and not get bored.

This is a place you might hold a story in your hands, a place that might take your story and hand it back to you at peace.

I would like to tell you more about Otis, but I am hesitant too, for everything I say about him is something I should know about you and don't, something I would know, I cannot make up for, something I must let go of as I cannot change it.

Jump-cuts

MY RIGHT LEG ACHES MOST days, along that large muscle at the front of the thigh. Sometimes it's as if someone unscrewed it from the hip in the night and screwed it back on but cross-threaded. If I swim or cycle, I feel my whole body bunch up on the right side, containing me, as if I might spill out otherwise. I don't walk straight.

The physiotherapist who told me to stop sleeping like Superman gave me a little blue ball with soft plastic spikes that recall instruments of torture. Some nights I lie facedown on the ball, positioning it at the trigger point at the top of my right leg where it hurts most. I roll it down the muscle, find the lumps. The pain is intense.

My right leg remembers. It twists and turns and wakes me in the night. When it stops aching it leaves a searing hot pain in the large muscle that covers my heart from behind.

⌇

We come to the things I am hesitant to write about. There are a number of reasons, themselves not easy to articulate. They say the past is another country and we surely are another race within it. I can no more understand the teenage me than I can understand people who are speaking a language foreign to me. Even less can I understand what motivated someone else, what motivated my teacher, her husband. How can I hope to make someone else understand?

I am used to doing two sorts of writing: corporate writing, where I make facts seem believable, and creative writing, where I make fiction seem believable. This writing is different. I am not seeking to make anything believable and these are the slippery sort of facts that depend so much on where you see things from. I am struggling here for I want most of all to be truthful.

Telling the truth does not mean I will be objective. In fiction, we talk of the point-of-view character, the character who mediates the words and actions of all the other characters in a story. Some point-of-view characters are notoriously biased. Others tell bold-faced lies. Even the relatively harmless can only see the world through their own eyes. I am the point-of-view character in my story and can only see what I have seen. I am truthful but truth is rarely objective.

There are things that concern my teacher's husband, and it may be they are better left unsaid. I cannot know. I can only go blindly into this place.

And there is fear, and fear is real. Fear is always real.

⌒

I have no recollection of when my teacher's husband started touching me. I only have these scenes that jump-cut to other scenes. This is common, I read later in my life. We deal with trauma by breaking it into manageable bites and storing those. We bring them out when we can deal with them. Some parts of that period of my life have not come back, may never come back.

The City Botanic Gardens. We are lying down on the riverbank and kissing. He has his hands down my pants and I am dizzy and nervous. Constitution Hill, on the way home from his parents' house. We kiss and he touches me. The footbridge near Marist Brothers. He is dropping me home from their place. We have pulled over and we are kissing. I don't remember enjoying these experiences. I like the power I have, or think I have. And I am curious. I want to see what will happen.

At some stage, my teacher guessed what we were doing—we came home with grass in our clothes—and at that time I think she might have wanted to put a stop to it. She went to see my mother. She said I was a nuisance, wouldn't leave them alone, and that Mum should intervene. She told Mum she was worried about what people would think of me running around the yard with her husband in nothing but swimming togs. Mum did speak to me about it, said I shouldn't be spending so much time with them, but she had no idea what was really happening and I ignored her, told her I was going somewhere else when I went to their place.

My teacher told her husband she'd been to see Mum. He fixed it, he told me afterwards. He told her that we shouldn't end a good friendship, that what happened was understandable—we were spending so much time together and we were all so close; he and I fell off the rails was all—and that it wouldn't happen again, that I was in trouble and needed them in my life to help me. My teacher accepted this. She contacted my mother and said not to worry. Her husband said we mustn't kiss anymore.

When I was a teenager, before I knew my teacher and her husband, John Denver became one of my heroes. I bought his records. I bought a book about him. I learned to play his songs on the guitar. I remember the book said his vocal range was an amazing two and a half octaves. It suggested if you wanted to understand what that meant, you should try to sing along with 'The Eagle and the Hawk', so I tried and found I couldn't.

In year eleven, my class went on a camp to Binna Burra in Lamington National Park. My parents had never been national park people. I doubt we ever bushwalked together. But when I went into that rainforest for the first time—the play of light, the density and range of greens, the smells of humus and life abounding, the peace of those massive trees—I knew I was in a spiritual place, the place where creation belongs. John Denver was somehow part of this spiritual place for me.

In my twenties, I was too cynical for John Denver, disbelieving for a time in the goodness of the world that had been the core belief of my life. I commented wryly on his drinking, his philandering, his golf-playing. He became the butt of my jokes. In my early thirties, I went to see him in concert. He was not my hero anymore and his stylised country shirts with gold embroidering and his white slacks and shoes were not the clothing the protector of Alaska I recalled and loved would have worn.

Just lately, though, I have been listening again to John Denver, liking what I liked in the first place, the simple trust expressed in his songs. He wrote beautiful songs: 'Leaving on a Jet Plane', 'Starwood in Aspen', 'Rocky Mountain High', 'The Eagle and the Hawk'. They are songs that celebrate the natural world and the human spirit within it.

I used to buy John Denver records for my teacher. We would play them together and listen to the words. I believed she knew what it meant, that connection John Denver had with the natural world, the spiritual world. I thought she understood in a way no one else did. One weekend, her husband was away on an exercise. I'd told her about the biology camp at Binna Burra, how it had affected me. On the Sunday, she drove me up to Binna Burra and we went walking. Later, in a pottery course, she made a vase that looked a bit like a tallowwood trunk and gave it to me.

⌒

Later in year eleven, after my teacher's husband and I resumed kissing, I started sleeping in their bed with them. This was his idea. We'll all cuddle, he said. I was eager. I longed for more of my teacher's attention and affection. I would have done anything for her. My teacher went along with her husband's suggestion. I don't know if she was keen or reluctant; perhaps she was both.

In their bed, it was cuddling at first, but the cuddling quickly became sexual. They both touched me. When one was touching me, the other slept or pretended to sleep, as if they didn't know what was going on. I learned a lot about sexual contact, had orgasms, although at the time I didn't know what they were. There was no intercourse. I touched both of them as well. I learned what you do. They knew all about it. They taught me what you do.

We never discussed what was happening among the three of us. I had sexual experiences with my teacher or with her husband and they didn't talk about it in my hearing. They had sex during this time, as far as I know, although I was never involved. When I was in their bed, I was in the middle. They would touch me all over and sometimes I became so excited it felt as if I'd explode.

I know my teacher and her husband talked between themselves about the sexual touching they were doing because he told me that one night they decided one of them would touch the top half of me and the other would touch the bottom half. He told me this as a joke. He thought it was funny. I remember the night he was talking about. I was terrified their hands would find each other's.

When I was in therapy in my late thirties, I couldn't write about what happened with my teacher and her husband and the therapist suggested I draw something, since drawing was less contrived for me. I am good at tricking people, even tricking myself, with words. I'm not so good with drawing. I drew three people in a bed, the middle one curled up. Then I drew a winged creature leaving the bed. I could not get up from that bed on my feet. I could only do it with wings.

When my teacher and I talked, it was guilty talk, what terrible wrong we'd done. She went to see a priest and confessed. She sent me along to the same priest and I confessed. Homosexuality. That's what we confessed. The priest told me it was a sin but many women committed it.

My teacher and I agreed it wouldn't happen again and then it happened again.

With my teacher's husband it was different. He called what we were doing the naughty but nice things of life, said we weren't harming anyone else, said it was better for me to learn about sex from good people than from some pimple-faced idiot.

⸺

During year twelve at Saint Catherine's, I started to resent my teacher's husband's control over my life. The strong views about the world that had reassured me now started to feel suffocating. You weren't allowed to disagree. He started to express strong views about what I should do. He believed my parents were not good parents, which I came to resent. He called my father a cuckoo when I told him that Dad didn't like him, didn't like me spending so much time with him. He said my parents set a bad example. They smoked. So did I. He hated smoking. He said they hadn't taught me manners. Sometimes I argued with his strong views. Mostly I didn't. I came to feel ashamed of my family, ashamed of who I was.

I met up with one of the girls I'd been friendly with at All Hallows', Marlene, who'd become involved in drugs, marijuana and a thing called Dutch acid which I assume was LSD by another name. Without meeting her, my teacher's husband took a dislike to Marlene. It made me like her even more. I missed days at school and went to Marlene's place.

Marlene and her brother were bright and I loved being with them. We listened to music together. We listened to Rodriguez. We thought we knew something. We could never quite articulate what it was we knew but that too was okay. It was different having friends my own age again—friends who, like me, didn't know everything, who were searching.

Marlene got some marijuana for me to take on a school camp. Soon after, her house was raided by the drug squad. In an interview, she and her brother were accused of selling drugs to school kids (Marlene finished a year ahead of me because I repeated), which would involve much more serious charges than possession. Marlene was convinced it was me who contacted the drug squad since they knew she'd sold drugs at a school and I was the only one of us whose house wasn't raided. No amount of protest from me convinced her of my innocence. She is a social worker now, I believe, working with street kids. She has not spoken to me since what she believed was my betrayal.

My teacher's husband told me he didn't contact the drug squad. I believed him, although I now see that he was the only one with the information. He was a freemason and often mentioned the contacts he had in different places. Then he told me he did ring the drug squad but only after Marlene and her brother had been charged and only to make sure they didn't raid my house. He vouched for me, he said, rescued me, but he wasn't the one who told the drug squad about Marlene. Someone else did that, he said.

My teacher's husband didn't like Marlene, didn't like me spending time with her. He would have told himself he was protecting me from drugs. He would have told himself he was doing the right thing. He had strong views about right and wrong. Even now, I find it hard to believe he lied to me, but of course he did. He called the drug squad and I lost Marlene, my only friend other than him and my teacher.

By the time I was finishing year twelve, I was spending every spare moment with my teacher and her husband. I missed days of school. I remember my teacher dropping me off one midday, a few minutes late for an exam, down the back of the school so no one would see. I was worried I'd fail the exam. 'What have you got to worry about?' she said. 'Just think about this: you conquered your teacher.' I'm sure this is how she saw what had happened.

Except for the sexual contact, our relationship was a friendship, although it must have looked odd to some people. I was a teenage girl and they were a couple in their late twenties. We went to the beach, we went on walks. They were older, more responsible. I viewed them this way. They viewed themselves this way. I met their families, their friends. I was introduced as a girl from the school. They were helping me. That's what people thought. I was troubled and they were helping me. It was what I thought. They were more like parents to me than friends.

At the end of year twelve, when all of the finishing high school students go to the coast, my teacher and her husband came to the beach where I was staying with girls from my class. We were lying on the beach at night and my teacher and I were touching each other and her husband was pretending to sleep on her other side and he sat up and said they should go home and she said it was up to me. I said for them to stay.

When I got back to the apartment where the other girls were staying, I felt like an alien. This was the way I felt among my peers in those months. We were no longer the same. These were girls with boyfriends and lockets, who had no experience of the things I was experiencing. I felt different, superior, like I knew everything that mattered, but also estranged, untouchable. I had nothing in common with these girls anymore and, although I didn't know it, I could never go back to being among them.

⌒

In my last months of high school, I applied for a cadetship in journalism with Queensland Newspapers. I was offered a position at the afternoon daily, *The Telegraph*. When I finished school, I started in Women's News, run by the formidable Miss Erica Parker who, in addition to editing Women's News for the paper, also wrote her own daily column, 'Parker Point'.

For a Girl

Before I started at the paper, my mother took me into
the city to buy grown-up clothes: a pleated grey skirt and
blouse, a blue dress with a red tie at the front, pantihose,
bras—things I'd never worn. Except for school uniforms,
I still wore pants; not my brothers' hand-me-downs anymore
but jeans and t-shirts. I went to work in my new clothes and
felt like a grown-up.

Miss Parker had dyed bluish hair in a bun that looked
so tight it lifted the flesh around her eyes. She wore thick
eyeliner and eyeshadow matching her eyes. She chain-
smoked. I soon learned that when the sub-editors changed
her prose as a columnist, which is their job, Miss Parker
would change it back when she got the pages to proof as
Women's News editor.

Other cadets had to circulate through different areas—
sport, general news, the television guide. But I wouldn't have
to do that, Miss Parker said in my first month. I would just
stay with her. I admired her. Within a month of starting,
I was writing feature articles on issues I was interested
in. I wrote a story about skincare products and how they
have no evidence base, another about intelligence and how
it's measured. Miss Parker sometimes gave me a by-line.
There would be the headline on the story and then it would
say 'by Mary-Rose MacColl'. And then there would be the
words I'd written.

I stayed out of the darkroom. My colleagues in Women's
News warned me that the picture editor was a groper. I went

to the compositors' room where they set the news in lead on the big linotype machines. I talked to the men who worked with my father, who said if I was lucky I'd be a chip off that old block. I went to the presses to see their fabulous machinery turning out thousands of newspapers.

I was spending less time with my teacher and her husband now that I was working, more time with my work colleagues. Soon I would be at university, studying the journalism degree that was a requirement of my cadetship. I talked to my friend Jessica's father who was a bank manager about borrowing money to buy a car.

As I write this now, I wonder how my life might have been different. If I hadn't had you, would I have come to see my teacher and her husband through different eyes? Would they have faded like other heroes and become just ordinary? If I hadn't had you, would everything have been different, and is this an all right thing for me to think about, or should I only be thankful that you were born, that you live and breathe in the world somewhere?

I am thankful that you live and breathe in the world somewhere.

After my loan was approved, my teacher's husband arranged for me to buy the car from a friend of his who had a car yard at Redcliffe. Once I had my own car, I wanted to drive around by myself, but my teacher's husband said I shouldn't drive on my own until I was more confident behind the wheel.

On Anzac Day, I was picked to cover the dawn service and parade for *The Telegraph*. They sent me, a cadet with a few months' experience, rather than a more senior journalist. Miss Parker said this was because the stories I'd been writing in Women's News had been noticed and so now I was being entrusted with an event of great importance in the general news area. She said I must watch carefully.

I picked up the photographer before 4 am and we drove into the city and parked in a no-standing zone using our *Press: Please Pass* dashboard card. The photographer was grumpy at first to be going out so early and we didn't talk much on the way. Normally he would have driven—photographers drove reporters, not the other way round—but he'd lost his licence for drinking and driving and so he had to put up with being driven around by a girl. Even driving *The Telegraph* car felt like a mark of trust.

We arrived at the service and they played 'The Last Post' and then there was the silence. I was crying. 'Isn't it beautiful?' I whispered to the photographer after the silence ended. He went to say something but stopped himself when he saw my face, nodded instead and smiled at me. On the way back to the office, he told me I did a good job, said the piece I'd written about Simpson and his donkey—I'd found a modern-day Simpson with a modern-day donkey and phoned it in—should run on page one. It didn't run on page one.

It was on page twelve, at the bottom, with my photographer's excellent picture.

⸺

One night, my teacher's husband and I went to visit his friend who had the car yard, the one I'd bought my car from. There may have been something that had to be added to my car, I don't remember, but my teacher didn't come with us. The friend had been in Vietnam with my teacher's husband. It was a special bond, my teacher's husband said, one I wouldn't understand. After we'd visited his friend, we all went to drink at a hotel. I drank a lot of beer. My teacher's husband was driving my car. After we left his friend, he drove me to the beach. It was dark. He kissed me, touched me.

For twenty-five years I remembered it this way. We had too much to drink. We went off the rails, over the edge, did the naughty but nice things.

My right leg aches and aches until one afternoon, when I am on the floor crying and afraid, there is another remembering.

The man and girl are on the beach and they are kissing and he is touching her and she him. And he is moving now, taking off her jeans, her pants, his own, and she is saying stop we better stop, she is laughing as she says it but her laugh is shallow, nervous, like her breathing, and he is saying it's too late it's too late and he is on top of her and she is yelling now to stop and she is pushing her right leg against him, she is trying to kick, she is crossing her right leg over her left but she is not strong enough his arms are holding her, his legs are holding her in place and he is hurting hurting hurting she is young younger than you think and it is done.

And then I am alive and I am shaking and crying and cannot stop.

My body knows

IT WAS A SATURDAY MORNING a month and a half later and I was with Wendy, my friend from All Hallows'. Like me, Wendy left the school in year ten. I hadn't seen much of her, but she'd phoned me a few weeks before out of the blue and suggested we go and see Sister Maureen, our old maths teacher, who'd left the order to marry a widower with five children. We didn't have to call her Sister Maureen anymore, Wendy said when we were on our way. Now we could just call her Maureen.

I wanted very much to see Sister Maureen who was from my old life. I was feeling so afraid.

During the week, I had taken a specimen of urine to a pharmacist. Three days, the pharmacist said. Saturday was the third day. I asked Wendy to stop so I could make a call. I didn't say who I was calling. I rang the pharmacist. He said, 'Congratulations, you're going to have a baby.'

The light was soft as it often is in autumn in Queensland. The sun had started on its journey away from us and even the Pacific Highway, one of the ugliest roads on earth, looked at ease, ready to receive us. I lay down outside the phone booth on the hard brown grass next to the highway, staring up at the blue sky.

It was as if my body knew something my mind did not.

Wendy wanted to know what was wrong. 'Someone died,' I told her.

'Were you close?' she said.

'I don't know.'

We visited Maureen but I couldn't get my head around her name. I kept calling her Sister: yes, Sister; thank you, Sister; no thank you, Sister. She laughed when I did this. She mothered five children now; she was no longer Sister. She had such a lovely laugh. Sister Maureen served tinned asparagus, which I'd never eaten. I've never forgotten the taste. Every time I eat tinned asparagus, I am back there. Sister Maureen beamed at us and said, 'Look at you, you grand girls. I always knew you'd make good.'

I had turned eighteen just a few months before. My colleagues in Women's News bought a cake and sang: Janne, who did the fashion; Elaine, who wrote features; and Miss Parker herself, who had been so kind to me. All of them kind.

I was eighteen, an adult. I had been feeling so grown-up. But now I was feeling very small.

I didn't think of you. I didn't think of you that day, nor any day through the long months we spent together. I didn't think of you. I went home and told no one. I made plans to go somewhere else. I told myself I would go somewhere and have it and give it up. I called you 'it' in all the time we were together. To be honest, I had no idea who or what you were.

My teacher and her husband guessed. They forced it out of me one night the following week when I was at their house. I had said I might leave my job as a cadet journalist—I couldn't think what else I'd do—and they wanted to know why. I was in a big lounge chair curled up small and they leaned over me, one on either side, and demanded to know what was going on, demanded that I speak. I was shaking all over, wanting to disappear. The shame I felt. This was all my fault, I was sure. The beach, the night I drank too much. We did the naughty but nice things. We succumbed. I burst into tears and told them. I sobbed and sobbed and sobbed.

They told me not to worry. They would fix it.

The next day, my teacher's husband contacted a priest, an ex-army chaplain in Melbourne, who knew of a home for girls where I could stay. We agreed I should go away. Melbourne was a city they knew well that I'd never seen. Our family went to Sydney once, towing a caravan, when I was twelve, but other than that we'd only been close to Brisbane for holidays. My teacher and her husband told me it would be an adventure. I believed it would be an adventure. They would come down for the birth, they said. They would visit me and everything would be all right.

Over the next week, I told everyone I was going to leave my job as a journalist. I was casual in the saying of it, didn't tell them why. I said I wanted to travel. This was shocking to my parents, to Miss Parker. I had been one of four successful applicants for cadetships from among more than four hundred who applied, Miss Parker said. How could I throw that away? She couldn't understand me.

My teacher and her husband talked, but I was not included. My teacher was unwell, an unspecified unwellness later diagnosed as endometriosis. They had no children. My teacher's husband called them brats, said he didn't want to end up like his siblings who had brats. He told me I had upset my teacher. I felt bad for what I'd done, what I'd done to my teacher. She wasn't harsh with me but I was sure she blamed me. I blamed myself. It was all my fault and I had to make it right. We agreed it would be best to keep my pregnancy a secret from everyone but my family.

We also agreed that while I should tell my parents I was pregnant, I shouldn't tell them my teacher's husband was the father. If people knew, the scandal would cost him his commission as an army officer.

My mother had guessed about the pregnancy as soon as I announced I was going to quit the job I loved so much. More to the point, first thing every morning I vomited. When I told her the father was a journalist I met at a party, she went very quiet and looked hard at me.

'I was drunk,' I said, 'and I don't know his name.' I closed my mouth and set it tight. I would not say more.

My father pushed until my mother turned to him and said, 'That's enough, Mac.'

Strangely, of all the things I later worried about, this was the worst: that I agreed to tell my mother I became pregnant when drunk, having sex with a man whose name I couldn't remember.

⌒

My parents would have been happy for me to stay in Brisbane instead of going away to Melbourne. We were not a family that had the luxury of caring much about its reputation, and Catholic Church rules were the least of our failures of social expectations. My father's family's Catholicism was two generations back. His French grandmother had been devout. Dad always claimed to be without religious beliefs, atheist not agnostic, any time I asked him. He may have converted to marry Mum, but he was just fibbing if he did. Mum was softly creative and flexible in a family full of Catholic pragmatists, run staunchly by Nana, who took charge of her children's affairs her whole long life. Nana was a devout Catholic, attended Mass every morning, and told me to take the confirmation name Josephine so I'd have a peaceful death.

'You don't have to go away on our account,' Mum said. 'Only if you'll feel better.' She looked at me again. I thought she might be going to say more but she didn't.

By this time, the Catholic Church had already started to change anyway, to modernise. Girls who got pregnant were not wicked in those days; they were stupid. There was good contraception, family planning clinics. We were not bad, except in the eyes of one or two old ladies and the conservative end of the Church, which was losing ground.

While contraception and abortion remained mortal sins, there were priests who took a broad ethical view, who accepted that divorcees might remarry, who baptised the children of non-Catholics, who were kind in the face of sin. Most young women wouldn't have thought twice about going on the pill. Priests and nuns were leaving in droves, pairing up and making new lives. I was not the mortal sinner that girls who were pregnant a decade before were, but I was not a good person either. I was a dolt.

Of course I had to go away. My teacher and her husband had said if anyone knew about the pregnancy, he would be in trouble. Other people didn't understand. Of course I had to go away.

Before I left *The Telegraph* I told Miss Parker I was pregnant. She had been miffed when I gave her my letter of resignation, citing no reason other than a desire to travel, so I told her the story I'd told my parents.

Then she was annoyed with me all over again. 'That was stupid,' she said. 'Very stupid. You are a little fool.'

She meant getting pregnant. She meant throwing away my career, because she could see, as I couldn't, that I would not get it back. She wanted to know who the journalist was, the father. I said I didn't know.

Even if she called me a fool, Miss Parker understood my leaving. The world was starting to change, but leaving was what girls had done for years in Brisbane and Miss Parker was on the conservative side of conservatism.

She asked if she could tell the editor of the paper. I said she couldn't. I was worried for my teacher and her husband. The more people who knew, the more likely he'd be in trouble.

Miss Parker shook her head, called me a fool again, and said to come back when it was over and she'd see what she could do.

⌐

My father wanted us to have a conversation about abortion. I'd resigned and was about to leave for Melbourne. Dad had been asking why I couldn't tell them the journalist's name, why I didn't remember.

'Shouldn't we find him?' Dad said to me, to Mum.

'I do not want to find him, no,' I said.

Dad said to Mum then, in my hearing, 'I don't see why she can't just look after it.' At first, I thought he meant the baby; look after the baby.

I was silent.

Mum said, 'Mac, she can't do that.'

When I realised he meant have an abortion not keep a baby, I left the room in tears, not because of any regard for the child growing inside me, but because I had been to the seminars at school run by Right to Life. They turned out the lights in the concert hall at All Hallows' so we could see properly. They showed us hundred or so schoolgirls the slides they brought with them in their carousel, the tiny perfect feet between a finger and thumb proving categorically that life begins at conception, the burgeoning foetus at time of termination. They told us about the different methods used and how much pain the baby felt. The suction method, the saltwater death, the poisons. I had been told about the evil of abortion. I knew it to be murder. I would never have an abortion, I told my father.

A year later, when I became pregnant again, I had an abortion without hesitation.

101 Grattan Street

I LEFT BRISBANE AFTER I finished up at *The Telegraph* and drove my car to Melbourne with my oldest brother, Ian. Crossing the border from New South Wales to Victoria at 3 am, I was spooked by big gums hanging over both sides of the highway at Echuca. I was as far from home as I'd ever been. Ian was asleep on the back seat and I couldn't rouse him no matter how hard I tried. I longed for a human voice, so I turned on the radio and listened to country music. It was Johnny Cash, 'The Long Black Veil', which made me laugh—the reach of Dugald. At dawn, we had apple pie and cream and ice-cream for breakfast at a truck stop Ian knew from another trip.

For a Girl

At eleven o'clock that morning, Ian left me at St Joseph's Convent in Grattan Street, Carlton. He was going to stay with friends and then hitch a ride home to Brisbane. I remember I didn't want him to go; I stalled him with small talk at the gate, became close to desperate as he became keener to extract himself. Finally, he said he must go and off he went.

I waited a few moments more and then went up the path to the door and rang the bell. It was answered by a nervous-looking nun who took me into a parlour and said she'd get Sister Mary, who was in charge of the girls. The first nun made me a cup of tea. There were lemon crisp biscuits. I took two. She watched me eat them. I worried about the crumbs.

In Melbourne during that time, someone who caught the tram from the city, alighted at the corner of Swanston and Grattan streets and headed along Grattan would pass the Royal Women's Hospital across Swanston on their left. They would cross another street and then walk a little way further to 99 Grattan, which would be followed by 103, a double terrace, St Joseph's Convent, where the Sisters of St Joseph lived. That was the door I was told to knock on. There was no 101 Grattan Street.

But for years, 101 Grattan Street was where I thought I lived. It's where people addressed their letters to us girls. The nuns—whose terrace covered a double block—gave us that address so that there would be no real address if someone came searching for one of the girls. The postman knew the letters were to go to the convent at 103. The nosy neighbour or father-to-be might ring the bell at the convent and the nuns would tell them, 'No, this is 103. There's no 101.'

I only learned this years later, when I went back to Grattan Street with David, trying to understand something of what had happened, what I'd done. I went looking for the place I'd been and found it had never existed.

⌇

In the home, I had my own room with its own sink. I met the other girls, one of whom became my good friend. Jill was a nurse and the father of her baby was an apprentice from her home town in northern Victoria. He was young, like us. I told Jill the father of my baby was a boy I knew at university, also young like us. The father of Jill's baby came to visit Jill each month. They were going to be married one day, Jill told me, but not yet. They were not ready yet, their parents said. Same with me, I said.

Jill and I sat up late smoking cigarettes and drinking coffee. As our bellies swelled, we didn't talk about babies. We talked about what we'd do when we got out. We talked about the other girls. There was a girl we hated, Paula, who came back at the end of September, after her baby was born, much changed.

Paula was a chatterbox, never shut up—it was what we criticised in her—but when she came back to pack up after her baby was born, she had little to say. If this unnerved us, we never spoke of it. Later we heard she changed her mind and came back a second time, within the thirty days, and took her baby home. She changed her mind. Typical, Jill and I would have said, if we had said anything. Paula was weak.

Another girl, Jane, wasn't booked into the Royal Women's Hospital like the rest of us. She was a patient at the private Catholic Mercy Hospital. I think her people were unhappy about what she'd done. She was alone at St Joseph's. No one visited her despite the fact she came from Melbourne. She never mentioned her baby's father and we never asked.

Lily was a prostitute, pregnant for the second time, giving up a second baby. She'd had polio as a child and walked with sticks. When she was with us, we walked slowly. She said she didn't know if she would give up this baby.

When we went to antenatal classes at the hospital, we sat up the back of the room and giggled while the other women stretched and blew and panted on cue. There were men in the antenatal classes. They were the husbands of the women who were having babies. We were at the back of the room because we didn't have husbands. The husbands blew and panted too, as if the baby was inside them. We giggled more when we noticed this.

I never thought of the locals. Did people see us, pregnant girls in a line, and think we were the ones from the home, the ones without a man to speak for us? I didn't feel self-conscious or guilty, not then. If I felt bad, it was for what I'd done to my teacher. I was young enough to believe I was on an adventure, like my teacher and her husband said. My only cause for shame was what I'd done to them, what I'd done to my teacher. I felt it was all my fault. I'd ruined something for them.

I went to the zoo. I had only been to one zoo before, in Sydney on the family holiday when I was twelve. I drove to the Dandenong Ranges, going first in error to Dandenong the suburb, from where I could see the ranges miles away. I went into the city—it was such a big city—and wandered the shops.

As my belly swelled, I began to see it as a lump, an inconvenience, that stopped me sleeping. Not as anything else. I never looked at books with pictures of babies in them. I didn't notice if ever I happened upon a woman with a baby in the street. I didn't see women with babies at the hospital when I went for appointments.

⌐

Sister Mary told us that an occupational therapist was coming to see us on Thursday mornings. She was blonde, the occupational therapist, and worked hard to act as if we were normal. She smiled and trained her eyes on our faces, ignoring our bellies. In one of the first sessions, I said, 'Are we going to do basket weaving?' She told me I could leave if I wanted to, so I did. I went and hung around Sister Margaret in the kitchen.

Sister Margaret was the cook at St Joseph's. She cooked for the nuns and for us. 'The same food,' she told me. 'I cook the same food for you as I do for us. I don't let them do the other.' She didn't tell me what the other was. I think it was that the nuns would eat different food from the girls. This is what they did in some of the girls' homes. The girls ate poorer-quality food.

In some of the homes, girls were made to work. At St Joseph's, before my time, girls were made to work. The nuns took in linen and the girls washed it and wrung it out to earn their keep while they waited for their babies to be born. They were treated as unforgiven sinners. That was why their food was different from the nuns' food. Their sin was not that they were going to give up a baby. Their sin was the sex that made the baby. Giving up the baby, sending the baby to a good home with two Catholic parents, was what redeemed them, got them out of the home where they were sinners unforgiven. It got them forgiveness which was worth having.

The memory of these beliefs was still fresh when I was in Melbourne. There were still nuns living in the convent and this was their view, including Sister Mary, who looked after the girls. She liked me, because I was intelligent and read books. I think she might have found my behaviour hard to square away with who I was, would have preferred, I think, sinful girls to be unintelligent. It was such a sad place when I think back now.

I liked Sister Margaret best. She was tall and large-boned, in her fifties when I met her, the youngest of twelve children. She told me that when her father died she was not allowed to go home to attend the funeral, so when her mother died she didn't ask; she just said to her superiors that she was going. They said she had to take a chaperone. She took an eighty-four-year-old nun who had no idea who or where she was. Sister Margaret sat the old nun in a chair and left her there while she mourned her mother's passing with her siblings.

Sister Margaret had a red face, as if her heart was about to let her down or she'd just come in from a windy walk along a headland. She added so much salt to our food that sometimes it was hard to eat. 'I have to cook it to someone's taste,' she said, 'so I cook it to mine.'

When we met up again in later years I felt uncomfortable around Sister Margaret but was unable to articulate why. Eventually I stopped replying to her letters and we lost touch. I kept a coffee mug she gave me, beige Dunoon porcelain with brown sheep embossed on it. I've tried to throw it out several times, but it keeps getting out of the bin and up onto the sink, so I've given up.

I was living on sickness benefit, the only support available to pregnant women. I bought vitamin E because my teacher and her husband told me to take it for my skin, so I didn't get stretch marks. I got them anyway, long red welts across my breasts and down my belly. I bought cigarettes and toiletries. I shopped at King & Godfree. Some nights the other girls and I went down Lygon Street and bought pizzas. I went to the cafes my teacher and her husband told me about. I went to Mass at South Melbourne, the parish of the priest who found the home for me.

His name was Father Bob and my teacher's husband knew him because he'd been an army chaplain. My teacher's husband rang him on my behalf and told him that one of his wife's students, a nice girl, had got herself in trouble and could Father Bob help. My teacher's husband told me this, that he had described me as a 'nice' girl. It was a joke. I was not a 'nice' girl, we all knew, because I was already in trouble at school before my teacher and her husband met me. They'd helped me get out of trouble. I was lucky they'd done this. This was what I believed. It's what they told me.

Where the real pain begins

Your other mother must have learned your name, Ruth, when the laws changed, because when I gave you up, they wrote to me and said their practice was not to tell the parents the baby's name given by the birth mother and not to tell me your new name. Your real name, they called it. They reissued your birth certificate too so that my name and anything about me would be gone from your life. You would only have your new name, your real name, as they said. That's what they did. It's what they believed would help us all.

The adoption agency, the Catholic Family Welfare Bureau, assigned me a social worker who came to see me once a week. Jenny Fish was a tall thin woman with a kindly nature.

I liked her very much, although I sometimes felt there was something she wanted to say but didn't.

Jenny Fish worked for the same organisation that found babies for childless couples. One of her colleagues would select my baby's other mother and father, she explained to me. There was a pool of other mothers and fathers by then because there were few babies and many infertile couples. They were screened, the other mothers and fathers, to make sure they were Catholic, financially secure and knew what they wanted. I would have a say in the matter, Jenny Fish said. She said this as if it would make me feel good. I had no idea why she'd consult me about anything.

In one of our first interviews, Jenny Fish asked me if I would want to know if my child died. I said yes, I would want to know but why was she asking me. 'I'd be allowed to tell you that,' she said. 'The courts allow me to tell you that.'

~

Mum and Dad drove down to Melbourne with my little brother Lachlan for Christmas. I hadn't seen anyone from home in six months and I was so happy to see them. The nuns lent us a terrace house they owned behind the home. I stayed in the terrace with Mum and Dad and Lachlan.

It was their first ever trip to Melbourne. I don't remember what we did. I was uncomfortably pregnant by then and had very few clothes. We may have stayed in the house mostly.

I think we went to the beach at Apollo Bay because Mum wanted to see the ocean. I just don't remember.

On the morning they were leaving, I didn't want to go back to the home. I was crying, finding it hard to manage. I hugged Lachlan, Dad and then Mum. I was crying and one of us made some inane joke which was our family's not very helpful way of dealing with emotional difficulties. It made me laugh through my tears.

Dad was backing the car, looking out the driver's window, and I saw in his eyes that he had begun to cry too. It was the only time in my life I ever saw him cry.

Now I can imagine what he saw: his young tomboy daughter in a polyester floral dress that might have suited someone twice her age, standing at the door of the terrace house. He reversed the car—a frog green Mazda 323 we owned at the time—into a drainpipe. He waved and pretended to smile, as if his tears weren't real.

I remember that smile, tears in his eyes, tobacco-stained teeth. I felt embarrassed for him, wished I could disappear.

My teacher and her husband had told me they would visit me in Melbourne. They would be with me for the birth. But my teacher's husband had had a car accident in their car and now it needed major repairs to the engine. As a surprise I sent my own car back home for them to use. I put it on the train and got Andrew to pick it up at the other end and put a ribbon on it and take it to their house. They really appreciated it, my teacher's husband said. I thought they could drive my car down to Melbourne and we could all drive home together.

When the time was getting close, my teacher's husband told me by phone that it would be too much for my teacher, who had been unwell. They wouldn't come and visit me after all.

I sent them a letter saying I felt angry that I would be on my own. Although I didn't tell them this, I had watched other girls go over to the hospital. They came back changed. I was worried. I wanted someone with me.

I regretted sending the letter almost immediately. I thought they would be mad at me for feeling as I did, so I rang and told them to rip up my letter without reading it. I was terrified that if they read it I'd lose them. And while I wasn't sure of anything else, I was sure I didn't want to lose them.

They didn't rip up my letter. My teacher decided to read it. She rang me, furious. 'How dare you?' she said. 'After all we've done for you. After what you've done to us.'

I capitulated immediately, dissolved into tears, went into labour.

Otis likes the idea that he has a sister and wonders if you are as good a teacher as Leah, who, as he's told me, doesn't ever get angry. When she tries, she just laughs. I have told him that I don't know what kind of teacher you are; I don't know anything about you.

There are things I remember. I remember in the morning my waters break over the bathroom floor. I clean up the bathroom floor, collect my bag, tell Sister Mary and walk across the road to the hospital like I've been told to do.

I remember that when the doctor examines me it hurts and when I flinch he smiles and says I have a long night of pain ahead.

The other girls from the home come over to be with me. I don't remember which ones, but Jill isn't there. She has already gone home, has rung me every week since to see how I'm going. The other girls and I go out to the visitors' area to smoke, but I have to excuse myself because of a feeling down there as if I might explode.

I remember my right leg is up in a stirrup. The midwife has put it there to get it out of the way. Only the right leg; they've turned me on my side to slow the birth because it's happening too quickly. I hear them say that. When the midwife lifts me, she says to the orderly on the other side of me, 'There's nothing to her under all that baby, is there?'

Then it's late afternoon, and I'm watching the sunset through large windows overlooking the city of Melbourne. A medical student with long brown hair and soft eyes comes to me while I'm eating ham sandwiches and says, 'I just have to tell you, that was the most marvellous thing I've ever seen.' He takes my hand, the one I need to reach the sandwiches. I have no idea what he's talking about, what he's seen that was marvellous.

For a Girl

I called you Ruth after the character in the Bible. I didn't think about the verse until just now. She's the one who says, Wherever you go, I shall go. Wherever you live, so shall I live. Your people will be my people.

I'm in a gynaecology ward. Someone tells me there's blood on the back of my nightdress. When I look in the mirror, I see that my hair is standing on end like the crest of a cockatoo. There are three other women in my ward. One of them had an irregular smear test and now has cancer of the cervix. She gives me cigarettes. When she leaves she hugs me and cries and says, 'I hope you'll be okay, honey.' I don't know why she's crying—she's the one with cancer—but I'm sure her tears are for me.

I have a picture of you, taken in the foster home. At least I think it's you. Your skin is wrinkled. Your eyes are red and puffy. You look like a wheezy old woman, wearing lemon booties and a lemon jacket. Do you know I smoked through my entire pregnancy and drank five cups of coffee every day?

I turn nineteen. The girls bring me a box of stationery they all chipped in for, with red-breasted robins on brown flowers. I keep the box for twenty years and then throw it out.

I went to see you, apparently. I remember walking along the hall with Sister Margaret. The hall has a beige floor which

89

curves up as a skirting for the wall. Sister Margaret is standing
to the left of me, so tall and solid in front of a sea of cribs, and
that's as far as I can go.

It is the third day after the birth, and I am crying. I cannot
stop my tears. They run down my cheeks and all over my
nightdress, bought especially for the hospital because the
booklet they gave us in antenatal classes said we should buy
a nightdress. I know what antenatal means now: it means
pregnant; it means before birth. Jenny Fish says these are
the baby blues and will pass. I am so convinced she is right
that when Otis is born, twenty-three years later, I will wait
in hospital for uncontrollable tears to start on the third day,
some hormonal kink in the birth system. But when Otis is
born, there will be no uncontrollable tears. Jenny Fish says
she hates to do this to me but I must sign the papers. I don't
stop crying but I do sign.

Some days Otis is a mouse and I am a mouse mother. Some
days he is a possum and I am a possum mother. This morning
he was a flipback whale so I was a flipback whale mother. For
whatever animal he is, I say, I am that animal's mother.

I know now what Jenny Fish always wanted to say but never
did. 'Don't give up your child.' She would have said it quickly,

furtively, and run out of the room, saying behind her, 'I have seen them later, girls like you. I know what happens to them. Don't let them take your baby.'

I am sorry, Miranda, so sorry for what I did to you.

PART II

Disappearing

A different skin

I DISCHARGED MYSELF FROM THE hospital in Melbourne as soon as I could stand up and spent two days in the home before packing and leaving. Sister Mary told me to wait until I was stronger but I didn't want to be there one minute more than I had to.

I had no clothes that fit my post-pregnancy body so I went into the city to buy a dress. I remember it was maroon with a black leather belt, a size twelve. Afterwards, I wore it to interviews until it became too big. I bought presents for everyone. I flew in my first plane.

Mum and Dad picked me up at the airport. It was so humid I felt like I was covered in honey. I was still bleeding heavily. My breasts had been bound in the hospital and I'd taken drugs to dry up the milk I was making. They were less sore but still engorged. I didn't say anything about what had happened. No one mentioned it.

My body was no longer me.

A few weeks after I arrived home, I saw a baby on the television. I felt as if I was going to be sick and ran out of the kitchen.

Mum followed me into my bedroom and found me on my bed crying. 'It will be like this,' she said.

'Like what?' I said angrily.

She didn't answer.

'Like what?'

She looked at me then and there was such sadness in her eyes, and such fear, I turned away from her, afraid myself.

I went to see Miss Parker. There was nothing she could do for me, she said. She had no authority. She suggested I go to see the editor. I did but he wouldn't give me a job.

'You threw us away,' he said. 'Forget it, kid.'

I applied for Melbourne papers but my applications were unsuccessful. I was interviewed twice, but they wanted to know why I'd left a good job and I couldn't tell them.

I applied for advertised jobs: writing copy, driving delivery vehicles, working in cafes. Australia was in an economic recession. I had no experience and no skills. I didn't get many interviews and if I did get an interview, I didn't get the job.

I started doing volunteer work with the Brown Sisters who nursed the sick poor in New Farm. I met their boss, Sister Katie Flannery, who taught me a lot about being among the unchosen. Katie was an alcoholic who hadn't had a drink for years when I met her. It was brandy, she said. Someone gave her brandy when she fainted and that was that.

I visited a family with Katie and she took a child in her arms and said, 'I was here giving food parcels to your grandmother and now I'm giving them to your mother. Will I be giving them to you too, or will something change?' She said to me afterwards that she thought nothing would ever change.

She was sick that day, from chemotherapy. We had to stop every few blocks so she could throw up in the gutter. She knew I'd had a baby, I think. Either I'd told her, or her friend Father Brian from St Vincent de Paul had told her. I got the volunteer work through Father Brian, and I'm pretty sure I told him about the pregnancy. It wasn't something Katie and I discussed, though, as far as I can remember. I know I didn't tell any of them who the father was.

The next morning the Archbishop came to the convent for breakfast—he lived just down the street and had a soft spot for the Browns—and Katie put his sultanas in an episcopal cross on his Weet-Bix. She nudged me under the table to point it out. It was hard not to giggle.

Except for my volunteer work I had no job that first year home. I had no friends, either, except my teacher and her husband, who I still believed were good to me, and one friend from school, Jessica, who was also volunteering for the Brown Sisters.

Jessica had been a good student, liked by everyone, the girl in the class you'd describe as a good old stick, even at seventeen. Her father was the bank manager who approved the loan for my first car. I hadn't told Jessica the real reason I left my cadetship in journalism. I'd said I felt like travelling. I wrote her from Melbourne, telling her I was working as a waitress, having a great time. While I was away, Jessica became friends with my teacher and her husband.

One Saturday, Jessica came to see me. She told me I needed to sort out what I wanted to do with my life. At the time, I was sure she thought me erratic, going to Melbourne for no good reason, coming home jobless. She said she'd be in touch. But I didn't hear from her. She didn't return my calls.

Later Jessica joined the Brown Sisters and studied medicine. Just before Jessica joined them, the other Brown sisters, the ones I'd known quite well who shared the New Farm house with Katie, cut me off. Katie was very ill by then, not working anymore, but I'd become close to some of the others too. They all cut me off, which was strange.

I never understood this. It was as if something had happened that Jessica didn't tell me about. For a time, I wondered if my teacher's husband said or did something to drive a wedge between us. Perhaps he did. But for me, it meant I had no friends. All I had was my teacher and her husband. And although I didn't know it at the time, I had staked my life on them.

⸜

My memories of my relationship with my teacher and her husband in the months after I came home from Melbourne are incomplete. I didn't sleep in their bed with them. That was something that stopped when I told them I was pregnant. We didn't speak of what had happened in the past. We didn't speak of stopping, although I do remember a conversation vaguely, when I went to talk to the editor of *The Telegraph*. We were laughing about his name. They were making fun of him and I was laughing along. It's very vague but it was a sense of making fun of him because he hadn't given me my job back, seeing it as his fault. It was that same feeling of superiority, that we knew something the rest of the world didn't, that we were special.

⸜

A few months after I arrived home, my teacher had to have an operation for endometriosis. She was in the hospital overnight. Her husband and I had been to visit her and then I went back to their house with him.

I have no memory of detail about this but I know we had sex that night on their bed. I know I was not forced. I know I went to the bed with him and had sex.

I was conscious of a body, but it was not mine. I remember he was on top and I was not in my body.

I was not using any form of birth control. This was despite the fact that a doctor in Melbourne had given me a packet of pills before I left the hospital. I threw it out when I was packing to come home. I remember how angry I felt when he gave me the pills. I didn't need birth control. I was not having sex.

And yet, I went to the bed with my teacher's husband and I had sex. I can't tell you why I did this; I don't know why I did it.

By this time, you could buy pregnancy tests that you did yourself at home. When I felt the familiar symptoms— sore swollen breasts, a missed period—I bought one, then a second, then a third pregnancy test. I remember the phials in my bedroom cupboard on a little stand. You collected urine in a dropper and put it in the phial with a chemical and waited two hours to see if a brown ring formed. A brown ring formed three times.

Without telling another soul, I went to see Children by Choice in Union Street, Taringa, so I could have an abortion. I used a false name. Abortions were illegal in Queensland in those days. The woman from Children by Choice arranged for me to drive over the border into New South Wales to a clinic at Tweed Heads. I stayed in the clinic while the sedative wore off, drove to a motel on the Pacific Highway at Burleigh Heads, took the pills they gave me to help me sleep and drank beer and ate ham sandwiches. I bled for three weeks and told no one what I'd done.

⌁

When I tell people I had a child long ago I gave to strangers, they sometimes say I did the right thing. And then then say, At least you didn't have an abortion. It reminds me what I did the second time I became pregnant.

I am not even that person, you see, the person some might admire, the person who didn't have an abortion. I am this other one, the person who did have an abortion.

⌁

Jill, my friend from the home, came to the Gold Coast in that year after we both left Melbourne. She and her boyfriend had split up, she told me. I drove down to see her. I said something along the lines of, 'Are you different now?' I wanted to tell her I was different. She was the only person I could tell. I understood it in my body but not my mind. In my mind nothing had changed. But my body was unmistakably different, like a beacon, the red stretchmarks on my belly and breasts, the scar where they cut me. Jill was on holiday with her nurse friends. She looked at me directly— she had lovely green eyes and a soft warm voice—and said,

'I'm getting on with life. That's what you have to do, get on with life.' I drove home and wanted to die.

⌒

I reached the bottom of my life that year. The second pregnancy gave me the energy to sever my relationship with my teacher and her husband, at least temporarily. Not because I thought they were bad, not then, but because I thought *I* was bad. I couldn't bear what I'd done to my teacher, and I couldn't bear the thought of being anywhere near my teacher's husband. I didn't tell my teacher and her husband why I wanted a break. I just told them I didn't want to see them anymore. At first, they left me alone.

⌒

Late in that first year home, I went on a reunion camp with the two priests who ran our senior religious camp at school. After the reunion camp, I went to the monastery at Oxley where the priests were staying and I told one of them what had happened between my teacher and her husband and me. I used the veil of confession, but I was telling him without their permission and this was the first time I'd breached our agreement of keeping the secret. I told the priest everything, about the pregnancies, the abortion, all the things I'd done. I was deeply ashamed, blamed myself entirely.

The priest did not vilify me. He listened. He offered me God's forgiveness. It was not solemn, his God's forgiveness, or ritualised. 'God forgives you, of course he does,' he said to me. 'But do you forgive yourself?' He agreed with me that it was probably best not to have too much to do with my teacher and her husband in future. He also said I shouldn't tell anyone else in the Church that I'd had an abortion. 'Not that what you did bothers God,' he said, 'but not everyone knows that God forgives.'

Coincidentally, the two priests who ran our reunion camp had also run camps at All Hallows', my old school, and at the camp I'd caught up with my old classmates from Saint Catherine's. I'd also met up with two girls who were a year below me at All Hallows', Louise and Lib. Lib and I had gone to the same primary school. They became my friends, my first new young friends since I became involved with my teacher and her husband.

Louise and I had six degrees of separation in our childhoods. We were both from biggish Catholic families, but hers had remained conventional whereas mine was out of kilter. Both her parents were accountants. Her father had a practice in the city. Nana knew their family, knew an aunt quite well. Perhaps they sang together. Louise's family had cousins out west who might have known Sing and Stacia, Nana's maiden aunts who ran the pub at Stanthorpe.

Louise and Lib were so normal. They were training to be nurses, saving up for cars, drinking rum and Coke and going to the beach every time they had four days off. They were interested in boys. They planned holidays. I didn't feel like them. I felt different, marked, but they continued to welcome me into their lives. The marks were on my body—I knew I couldn't let them see me naked—but also on my soul. These were harder to understand, to identify. I was so ashamed of what I'd done.

I managed to get a job in a nursing home as a nurse assistant. It was a difficult job, cleaning up old people, washing them, dressing them, feeding them, changing their beds. I loved Mrs Tilby, who would go from room to room stealing everybody's clothes and putting them on in layers, and her roommate, Mrs Bird, who was very grumpy with Mrs Tilby for not being able to behave herself. They were so wonderfully honest, these women at the end of their lives. I could listen to them for ages, as I helped Mrs Tilby remove layer after layer of clothing, which I'd then return to the owners.

Every now and then I went into a dark place inside myself. I drank myself into a stupor. I cut off from whoever I was with. I used to go to the pub with a couple of the nurse aides from work. I wanted to disappear. One night I found myself alone in the pub with no way of getting home. Everyone else had left and I'd said I was fine and wanted to stay on. Another night, I drove so drunk I could hardly see, didn't remember the next day how I got home, had to check my car was in the driveway to know for sure. On yet another, I slept in the gutter outside my house. I had no idea why or where these dark periods came from. All I could do was wait them out and go on with life.

In the first year after I came home, Jenny Fish and I wrote each other. She sent the signed *Form of Consent to Adoption Order*. With it, she sent a blank *Form of Revocation of Consent to Adoption Order*. This second one was the form through which I could change my mind, I knew, and withdraw consent to adoption within thirty days. I still have it.

In that year, I received reports on the baby's health and wellbeing. The reports told me many things: that the baby's posseting after feeds was settling down, that she was putting on weight now, that whenever her adoptive mother couldn't find her adoptive father, he was invariably in the nursery playing.

I would read these reports and they would mean nothing to me.

After a year, Jenny wrote and said she could continue to give me detailed information if I wanted, but some girls found it easier to move on if they didn't know anything. 'Do let me know your preference.'

I didn't reply. I didn't want detailed information. I didn't want to move on. I didn't want to know anything about any of it.

Byron sunrise

ALTHOUGH THE SUN HAS ALREADY risen, here at the farm it's still hiding behind the cloud on the hill on the other side of the dam. The sun's rays are forming a perfect semicircle out of the cloud and it's as if God, rather than the morning, is here to speak to me.

Someone on the beach at Byron will have watched the sun crack over the rocky outcrop of The Pass. It will have been sudden and less interesting than a few moments before, when the sea will have been in its predawn magnificence. Someone at the lighthouse will be scampering back down, having ticked the box 'Saw a beautiful dawn'. Someone on Mount Warning will be sending sun salutations to the morning.

Someone in Victoria, somewhere in Victoria, might still be sleeping, for morning comes later there. She will hear birds, perhaps, see black cows chewing green grass. She will have her own smell. She will be happy, I hope, contented with her life.

Those rays of light have narrowed and intensified now, although the sun is yet to appear. They are a beam from a light sabre that will pierce my heart.

Neither David nor I are redheaded and lately Otis has reached an age where looking different from us—everyone comments on his hair—is something he wonders about. He listens carefully as I tell him that David's mother Lorraine, who passed away before he was born, had red hair and that the men in my dad's family were redheaded Scots. I point to the red streaks at the sides of my head that came up like little devil's horns when I was pregnant with him, to the hairs under David's arms that are a red surprise.

He knows he is our child, but even so the colour of his hair has been enough to shake him.

It makes me wonder what it must be like to grow up without your kin, with skin or hair or eyes or anything that's different enough from the people who are otherwise your family that you don't quite fit with one another. I can't imagine it. My family was so much mine, all of us not quite like the rest of the world.

Keeping the secret

IT WAS A YEAR SINCE I'd arrived home from Melbourne. I'd broken from my teacher and her husband and I was starting to make new friends. I'd left the nursing home to take up a job as a boarding supervisor in a girls' school. I enrolled in a pastoral care course because the principal of the school was doing the course and she invited staff to attend.

I turned up on the first night of the course and there was my teacher. She'd moved from classroom teaching to a role designing religious curricula for Catholic school students. As part of her job, she had joined a team running a course for people working in helping occupations.

On the first residential weekend of the course, I saw my teacher at a distance but avoided her in person. I didn't want to talk to her, but at the same time I was also glad to see her. I felt she had something I needed, although I wouldn't have been able to say what.

I made friends with a young woman named Ann, who worked as a counsellor and had once been a nun. Ann was funny, especially about Catholicism, which she had so much modern experience with. When she met my friends, she pretended to be super religious, leading a group at dinner in prayer, getting us to join hands, everyone around the table going along nervously, then moving to praying in tongues so that no one knew where to look. She kept it up for ages before she burst into laughter.

On the first night of the residential weekend, Ann and I stayed up chatting. At some stage, she flicked some whipped cream from a bowl on the counter at me and I returned fire, and before long we'd wrecked ourselves and the kitchen. We cleaned it up as best we could and luckily no one needed the whipped cream for the remainder of the weekend.

Ann and I soon filled the role of difficult young students. I regressed to an earlier version of myself, playing up and disrupting the group I was in. I felt self-conscious with my teacher there. I didn't know who I was. I didn't talk to her at all, except to say hello each week. I was doing what I'd done in school, seeking attention.

Ann and I were separated, put in different groups, but it didn't stop me playing up. Eventually, the course director threatened to ask me to leave the course. I stopped playing up and finished the course, gaining nothing of any use.

⌒

I lived in the boarding house while I was on duty, so I'd have ten days on and then four or more days off. Sometimes I drove to Melbourne on my days off, although I didn't know why. I'd decide one day to go and leave the next. At least once, I drove there in one hit, leaving at midnight after a sleep so I could be there the next afternoon. I drove through the night with the stereo blaring. Another time, Louise and I planned to drive to Sydney on a long weekend, but we took a wrong turn and drove to Melbourne instead.

When I got to Melbourne, I didn't know what to do. I went into the city. I went to Carlton. I wandered the streets alone. And then I drove home.

⌒

Living in the boarding house felt strangely soothing. I think it reminded me of the home. I looked after years nine and ten girls who seemed decades younger than me.

One afternoon, I walked down to the river where the school had its boathouse. I could smell cigarette smoke. Two of the girls in my group came out of the boathouse. They looked frightened; they'd been caught smoking.

'Hello,' I said. 'Just look at those clouds.' I pointed. Saved by cumulonimbus, I imagine they thought, certain they'd fooled their stupid boarding supervisor. She must be a cloud nut!

These same students, two weeks later, were caught outside school without permission. They'd gone into town. I forget why. Perhaps we never knew why. But being outside school without permission had a penalty of immediate expulsion.

They came to my room, the two of them, after their parents had been called to come and get them. 'Please,' one of them said, 'they're going to expel us.' They'd come from the country to the school and now they'd have to go home. They were like young gazelles caught in a leg trap and in a panic. I felt awful for them. I said I'd do what I could.

I went to see the principal with whom I'd gone back and forth to the pastoral care course every week. 'I just want you to know,' I said to her, 'that if you expel them, you will end their chances in life. You will harm them.' It was all I could think of to say. There were no local schools that were as good as the school these girls were in. 'They are just really good kids, really good kids, and they've done one wrong thing.' They'd actually done many wrong things, but I didn't want to emphasise that.

The principal looked at me. I had spoken with considerable passion.

'You know,' she said, 'before we did the course I would have been affronted at your saying that. I would have dressed you down, a girl of your age thinking you know something.

But I can see this is really important to you, and I admire your wanting to help these girls. I really do.' She looked at me kindly. 'But I run a school for boarders. Their parents entrust me with their entire welfare. If girls leave the school, they are expelled. They all know this when they start. My hands are tied.'

I watched the girls pack their bags. They were angrier with me than with the school because they'd hoped I would help them and I hadn't.

'All best,' I said before they left the dorm. 'It's just another stage.'

They didn't believe me. I didn't believe me either.

⌒

A few months after the pastoral care course ended, my teacher and her husband turned up at a funeral. Sister Katie from the Brown Sisters had died of cancer.

I'd been to visit Katie in her last weeks. She'd asked for me and one of the other nuns called me. She looked at me—Katie had eyes that saw right through you—and said I didn't need to be forgiven. None of us did, she said.

I couldn't cope with her honesty or her dying. I left soon after, told her I'd see her again soon, knowing full well that I wouldn't.

My teacher and her husband didn't know Katie, but they came to her funeral with my friend Jessica. There was a lone piper playing 'Amazing Grace'. We sang 'One Day at a Time'.

Katie had asked her friend Father Brian to do the eulogy instead of the Archbishop. I don't remember what Father Brian said, except that he knew her and loved her and you could tell that.

Jessica left straight after the funeral, smiling sheepishly at me on her way out, but my teacher and her husband remained behind and we talked. My teacher suggested we go for ice-cream in New Farm Park and I said yes. Later, my teacher's husband told me he knew I'd be at the funeral and he'd wanted to see me.

I re-entered their lives. They re-entered mine. Just like that. There was no sex anymore, not ever again, but we acted like we were friends to one another. It was almost as if the things that had happened had never actually happened.

Later that year, my teacher and her husband went to live in Melbourne, where he was posted and she had a job in the Catholic Education Office. We remained in contact. I kept the details of what had happened between us a secret. I kept the secret.

People would ask me why on earth I left a cadetship as a journalist. I told them I left to travel. Where did you travel? Melbourne. I remember once someone laughing at me. They had expected me to say Europe, America, but all I'd done was go to Melbourne. These questions people asked about my past were excruciating for me. I had a secret. I hadn't meant it to be a secret, but once it was a secret, I couldn't tell it. And once I kept the secret for a little while, it sealed up behind me. It was impossible to go back.

Before I knew it, the person I had been became part of the secret too.

A lifeline

I QUIT MY JOB AS a boarding supervisor not long after the two girls were expelled. I knew they'd broken the rules but I didn't like what happened to them, and while being back in an institution had been strangely soothing, it was also unsettling.

I wanted a different job but the recession was worsening and jobs were more scarce than ever. I liked working with words and paper so I wrote around to government departments, colleges and universities—I rang them first to check they had a stationery department, figuring if an organisation was big enough to have a stationery department, it must do plenty of writing—and sent my senior results, references and an offer to do any job at all.

I got a response from the director of the External Studies Unit at Mount Gravatt Teachers' College. His name was John Schmidt and he was one of a number of people who threw me a lifeline in the next few years. When he interviewed me, he laughed. He had the loudest laugh I'd ever heard. 'You can hear him three offices away,' his secretary told me.

After I started work, John told me that my letter had been circulated to all the college's departments by the personnel clerk. John had seen my senior results, which were good, and moved heaven and earth to create a job for me. That was what he was like. He thought clever people could do anything. He didn't care that I'd left a cadetship in journalism either, something interviewers always asked me about. When he mentioned it and I stumbled, he just said people do odd things all the time and laughed his loud laugh.

John thought someone as clever as me could run his records system, which was precious to him, but after a few minutes of watching me try he decided I might be better suited to more basic tasks. I had no administrative experience and cleverness doesn't help in every situation. I sent his records system into catastrophic failure. They needed a computer person to fix it.

We played bridge every lunch hour because, as John said, sweeping his straggly blond hair back from his forehead, bridge was more important than life. It was certainly more important than lunch. I became a reasonably good clerk and a competent bridge player in External Studies.

After a month, I trained as a large-scale photocopier operator and it was here that I really found my metier. I could set daily copy targets and exceed them. I could spend all day reading the material the lecturers wrote for the distance education students. I was surrounded by words and paper, which I loved.

I sold my car—the one my teacher's husband helped me buy—to pay off credit card debts and bought a Datsun 1600 that had the motor of some other car. It felt like independence, which I badly needed, although the car had a number of problems.

I had several crashes in the 1600, one of which damaged the back door so much I had to tie it shut. One night, when the police picked me up for speeding, they saw the back door and they saw the ignition which hung under the dashboard. They took the car off the road and I was ordered to make it roadworthy or sell it. I did the latter, borrowed money and bought another car, a Mazda 626, a good car I owned for years.

The fact I could manage on my own to buy cars that worked was important to me. My teacher's husband had known everything about cars. It felt like a step away from him when I could choose and buy a car without his help.

I was still drinking to disappear. I left External Studies for a job as a computer operator. I enrolled in journalism at the Queensland Institute of Technology, converted to full-time study while still in a full-time job, got a part-time job to pay my debts. I did not want unstructured time, not ever. I filled every moment of every day with plans. I did not think of the past. I worked and worked and worked, and then I drank and disappeared.

⌒

Louise was the first friend I told a little bit of the secret. We were up at Mount Coot-tha, looking over the city of Brisbane. I said, quite suddenly and before I could think not to, 'Louise, the year before last, I had a baby and gave it away for adoption.' I called baby Ruth 'it'. I had never called her anything else.

In *Women Who Run with the Wolves,* Clarissa Pinkola Estés tells old stories she then analyses from a Jungian perspective. One is a story about secrets and what they do to us. A maid from a village is murdered by the woodcutter's son who buries her body in the woods. Reeds grow up from the place where she is buried and shepherds pull up the reeds and make pipes from them. When they play them, the pipes sing of the murder and the woodcutter's son is discovered. Estés says of secrets that they make us seal off parts of ourselves so that we can't live our lives fully. We can't live. Eventually, they come up out of the past like those reeds.

Telling Louise the first part of the secret was like the first reed. But secrets have such shame attached to them. I expected Louise would be disappointed in me. I thought I might even lose her friendship. But Louise was not disappointed. Instead, she became dearer, more loyal. She asked me what I had—it took me a moment to realise she meant what kind of baby— and I told her it was a girl. She put her hand on mine and said nothing.

I didn't tell all the truth, the truth about my teacher and her husband. It was enough that I had told her this much and she had not shunned me.

～

By this time, I'd moved out of home and was living in a flat with Ann, the young woman I'd met at the pastoral care course. She was working part-time as a counsellor, and I was working and studying.

My teacher and her husband came home to visit that Christmas. My teacher's husband had a fight with our land-lord, who was a difficult person. I don't remember the details of the fight—my teacher's husband may never have told me all of them—but Ann arrived home one evening to find that we had been evicted. Ann knew nothing about my teacher and her husband. She didn't even know I'd had a baby. Like everyone in my life, she thought they were older people who'd helped me. I was troubled, and they'd helped me.

At the time, my teacher and her husband were staying with his parents. They'd started a renovation on their Brisbane house which was unfinished. They'd raised the house and put in a slab underneath. My teacher's husband felt bad that he'd got us kicked out, he said. He said we could move into their house while they were in Melbourne for minimal rent. So we did.

The house wasn't easy to live in. Upstairs there were bedrooms and what used to be the lounge. Downstairs the floors were concrete. The kitchen was made up of old benches and makeshift shelves. It was a house that held memories for me, but I never noticed that.

My teacher's husband told me, on their visit to Brisbane the following year, that he could have finished the house and charged much more rent to someone, a family, but he wanted to help me after everything that had happened. He wanted to make up for what he'd done, he said.

A year later, Louise and Lib and I went on a driving holiday to Adelaide. We were passing through Melbourne on the way and we stayed a couple of nights with my teacher and her husband. I was relieved I had my friends with me. I felt uncomfortable with my teacher and particularly with her husband, although I didn't know why.

I didn't associate being back in Melbourne with the past. I didn't think of the past. I didn't think of the baby I had given away to strangers. It was as if the past me no longer existed.

By this time, my teacher and her husband had had a baby themselves, a girl. The baby was there with them, but I don't remember anything about her from that trip, just that my teacher was tired and in pyjamas all the time. They hadn't told me they were expecting a baby until late in the pregnancy. I didn't feel anything when they did tell me. I didn't connect their daughter with what happened to me. I didn't connect her with baby Ruth. I didn't think about baby Ruth, not ever. I remained disconnected from the person I had been.

I can tell you almost nothing about their daughter. She was a bright toddler, I think, although I've never met a dull one. I remember babysitting her when my teacher and her husband came to Brisbane to visit and taking her out to a friend's place, where she wouldn't settle to sleep. My friend said her mother would put rum in their bottles of milk with some sugar when they wouldn't sleep so I said yes, let's do that. I know I did this. I remember doing it. It confirmed something for me: that I was a bad person, an unfit person.

Thinking back now to just how much I was in denial during that time in my life, I am only grateful I didn't harm her more seriously. I was so disconnected from myself, I might have.

⌒

After we got back from Melbourne, I met a boy I liked, Simon, a friend of Louise's boyfriend Gerard. Simon's father's big sister had been a friend of my mother's at school.

Simon and I went out together as if we were normal young people. We went sailing, to concerts, bushwalking. Simon was studying. He used to come over to my place, my teacher and her husband's house, to study while I was at work and then we'd eat dinner and go see a movie.

Simon's family had casual Sunday dinners with their kids and their kids' friends. I didn't fit in. I felt exposed, like they knew me, knew how bad I was underneath. They were much more involved in the Catholic religion than our family. They valued intellect and discussed current affairs. I started going to Mass which I hadn't done for some years. Every Sunday morning, I read newspapers so I would know something about what was happening in the world in case I was asked questions on Sunday evening. I had no confidence. I was filled with shame.

At some stage, Simon and I decided we wanted to have sex but even this was full of shame. For me, there was no question of whether to have the light on or off. It could never be on because then he would know, when he saw the marks on my belly and breasts, that I'd been pregnant, that I'd had a baby.

I so much wanted to feel normal, like a girl who could choose to have sex. I went on the pill and I turned out the light and we had sex. But I was not there. I'd learned how to pretend to be there from television and movies, but I was not there.

Simon met my teacher and her husband when they visited. He said he was nervous about meeting them, more nervous than when he met my parents, because my teacher and her husband had been so important to me. He liked them and they liked him.

Eventually I told Simon I'd had a baby I'd given up for adoption. I didn't tell him who the father was. He broke off with me not long after and married a girl who suited him better. I'm sure it was hard for him to understand me. Even I didn't know what was happening. Sometimes I would drink until I couldn't think. Sometimes I'd withdraw from whoever I was with, and long to disappear altogether. I was frightened myself of what was happening and I didn't understand. How could someone else understand?

My teacher sent me a letter after Simon and I broke up. It was like a letter from a mother or an older sister. *Even if you and Simon love each other*, she wrote, *it is no guarantee you will make a good marriage together.* I accepted her advice, thought it wise.

⌒

Over time, the dark periods I experienced became more debilitating. I worked obsessively and drank, and worked obsessively and drank. I put on weight, took it off, took too much off, became a shadow, put it on again, became fat. I met the definition for anorexia, for bulimia, which I read about in a magazine. I didn't care. I liked the idea that I could control my body, which felt so far away from who I was, that I could eat or not and determine my size. It was a matter of control for me and I very much wanted to be in control.

Louise and Lib had no frame of reference to guide them on what was wrong with me, but they remained my friends.

They waited out my dark periods, when I withdrew from them and the world, and then they came back to me. I didn't know why they remained my friends through those years but they did and I am still thankful.

⌒

One night, while drunk and on my own, I cut myself up both arms, narrow stripes I made with a blade I'd broken out of a disposable razor. At work I had to wear long sleeves for weeks until the cuts healed. It really frightened me that I did this. I was worried about my drinking, which was out of control, but once I'd done this, hurt myself on purpose, I knew I needed help. I'd never heard of self-harming, but I knew what I'd done was the start of something frightening.

I found a counsellor, a social worker, through a youth worker friend who said he was great. His name was Mick and he was a big bear of a man who smoked cigarettes and ate meat pies for breakfast. He didn't care much about my drinking. He said he thought drinking was a way to deaden pain for me. He was more concerned about my working, he said. It was no wonder I needed to drink, given the pressure I put myself under. I worked long days, starting at 5 or 6 am and not finishing until after 7 pm. I was busy, always busy, always finding more things to do. I was studying full-time as well, trying to do as well as I could in a journalism degree.

Mick became impatient when I didn't make connections. I told him I'd had a baby and about the relationship with my teacher and her husband, but he concentrated on other things: on my family of origin, as he called it, on what Mum and Dad had done as parents, on my teacher and her husband as parents too, parents I'd given a special power to. That's how he framed what happened: that I'd given them special power and I could take it back.

I started having vivid dreams in which I was chased by a monster, knowing someone was in the house but unable to scream, trying to get away from someone who was catching up, catching up. I'd wake from these dreams sweating, my heart pounding, and remain awake through the dark hours. Some nights it took a long time for the panic to subside. Mick told me I was doing good work.

A few months into my therapy, I decided to break from my teacher and her husband. It felt different this time. It wasn't that I felt I was bad. I was starting to see that they were not helping me as I had believed. Although I had no idea yet what it had truly cost, I knew that our relationship hadn't helped me.

This was the first time I thought my teacher and her husband had done any harm at all. Until then, I believed I had done the harm to them. I am an otherwise intelligent woman, but I was unable to see something that other people have seen from the outset. Some people think I am unbelievably stupid. I am not.

I had already moved out of my teacher and her husband's house into an apartment with Lib. I didn't tell them I wanted a break; I just did it, stopped calling, didn't return calls. Eventually, my teacher's husband, who had always been the one to drive the relationship, stopped calling me too. It was such a relief.

Byron kindness

THIS MORNING I SWAM THE bay and thought I might die. I might die in the water, taken by a shark. The sea is so strange. We are a separate creature and yet part of the whole creature. We fear death and become part of death. I am terrified in the sea, terrified that I will end and by turns exultant that I am endless. A kayaker stopped beside me. 'Two dive boats are launching off the beach,' he said.

I looked and saw the dive boats. I couldn't work out why the kayaker was telling me about them, why he'd stopped in the middle of nowhere. He stayed beside me and it took a few moments more for me to realise he was watching over me so that the dive boats didn't run me over on their way out to sea.

'I'm a bigger shape than you in the water,' he said, smiling awkwardly.

I found myself crying into my goggles, having trouble treading water as I cleared them of my tears. I don't know what the kayaker thought of my crying. He remained with me, gazing out to sea, his paddle across his lap.

The dive boats whizzed past. The kayaker told me to have a nice one and paddled off.

'You too,' I called after him. 'You have a day of days.'

Ordinary men

WHEN DAVID AND I WERE first together, I would become frightened sometimes when we started having sex and I would ask him to stop. He always did and never seemed resentful. Once I asked him how he managed to stop when we were well on the way to intercourse. 'I just do,' he said, 'same as you.' But men can't stop, I said. They get to a point where they can't stop. This was before he knew anything about my teacher and her husband and what had happened. He laughed. 'Who told you that?' I didn't answer. 'That's crap,' he said. Then he looked at my face. I don't know what he saw, but he softened. 'I can always stop,' he said. 'It's all right. If someone told you something different, they were lying.'

After four years working at the college at Mount Gravatt, which by that time had joined Brisbane College of Advanced Education, I moved to the registrar's office, where I had a job writing reports about new courses for committees. I loved the quality of the debate among the academics, and I was still surrounded by words and paper.

I applied for a job running the council secretariat at the Queensland Institute of Technology down near Parliament House where I was still studying journalism. The job would involve writing minutes and correspondence for the governing council and its committees. It was a big promotion.

I got the job, reporting directly to the registrar, Brian Waters. After I started, I found out that when I'd applied, my former boss at the college—not John Schmidt, another fellow—was a referee. The council was the institute's governing body and important. He told Brian to get ready for some odd dress choices if he gave me the job. Brian told me this later. She might not be suitable for council, the other fellow had said. Brian said it had struck him as a strange thing to say and I'd interviewed so well and had such good references from the chairs of my academic committees that of course they were going to give me the job. I did have a pants suit that looked like pyjamas and baggy jeans way before they became fashionable; I'm sure Brian had noticed. But he didn't care, as long as I could think and write.

I worked closely with Brian and with the director of QIT, Dennis Gibson, a mathematician by training. He didn't care what I wore either. When QIT was becoming a university, I worked with the deputy director, Tom Dixon, on the submission to the state government making our case. Tom had run the school of communications, had developed the journalism course I'd done. He wasn't much interested in my clothes either.

I know these are just reasonable expectations of ordinary men, that they might focus on what a person can do rather than what they look like or what they wear, but it made a key difference to my life in the years I was working at QIT. I had dressed like a boy when I was young, and I had missed those years as a late teen when I might have learned to dress up and enjoy how I looked. I had no idea how to dress up and enjoy how I looked.

When university status was approved, Tom was acting director. I was the first person he came and told. 'Congratulations,' he said. 'You just wrote your first successful submission.'

⌒

I met David at QIT, where he was an internal auditor, working in the director's office doing organisation reviews. His undergraduate degree is in politics and the chair of the audit committee, an external member of council and government department head, had been surprised when he asked if anyone on the committee had read Machiavelli's *The Prince* and David had. The chairperson had hoped to bamboozle them with his knowledge of politics. The lowly administrator on the committee, who shouldn't know much, wrecked it for him.

When I wanted to review the institute's records management system, which was in my department, Brian suggested David would be the person to help.

While we were doing the project, I told David I knew all the words to Led Zeppelin's songs. It was during a conversation about memory, how strange it is what we forget and what we remember. It impressed him, that a girl could be so familiar with the music he loved.

On the corkboard in David's office I noticed a photograph of a leaf, a new leaf on a lilly pilly, sharply contrasted against a background of blurred green. He took the photograph in Lamington National Park, he said. He liked to walk there. Binna Burra was a special place for me too, I told him. It was clear to both of us we had things in common. We went to a concert in Brisbane together and held hands while James Taylor sang 'You've Got a Friend'.

～

Soon after we got together and before David moved in with me, I told him what I'd done as a teenager: my teacher, her husband, the two pregnancies. I knew I couldn't be in a relationship with someone unless they knew. I liked David, and even if it meant I would lose him, I had to tell him the truth.

I got Mick to help me prepare. I asked David over and said I had to tell him about something I'd done that was terrible. I sat on the floor of my bedroom with him and I told him everything. I was flat in the telling, could not look at his face. I was still so ashamed of myself.

'Is that all?' he said when I'd finished.

I nodded.

'It wasn't you that was terrible,' he said.

He held me for a long time. I was surprised by his kindness.

It was several weeks before I realised he wasn't going to leave me because of what I'd done. He didn't even see it as something about me.

Byron shark

NIGHT IS SO QUIET HERE at the farm that sometimes I can hear the wilder ocean on the Tallow Beach side of the lighthouse, heard first by the hill on the other side of the dam and then relayed to me. This morning, though, I cannot hear the ocean.

Last night I dreamed a man dressed in a rabbit suit came into our house in Brisbane and shot everyone but me. I don't remember who was there but I'm sure it wasn't David or Otis. They are still sleeping in the other room.

I half woke at first, my back locking up, a winch running through me from my heart to my hand. I couldn't breathe; the air would not go into my lungs. The man in the rabbit suit will kill me. That's what he has come for.

I had to wake myself up completely so I could breathe. I have been sitting on the veranda since then, waiting for the dawn.

When I was in Canada on a writing residency some years back, I had a lunchtime conversation with one of my colleagues, a poet whose sister had been murdered years before. We were at the Banff Centre for the Arts and our dining room window looked out to the Rocky Mountains I had always wanted to see. I looked at those mountains as my poet colleague told her story.

The poet was writing about her sister's death. She was worried that when her book came out, people would ask her questions she didn't want to answer. You can tell them it's fiction, I said—blithely, I realise now. For she could no more call her sister's brutal murder fiction than I can call what happened in my life fiction. You don't have to talk about the book, another colleague said. The fact you wrote it is enough.

I left the lunch table, blithe still, wondering why on earth my poet colleague was writing about what happened to her and her family around her sister's death. I thought she was too close to her experience, wouldn't do it justice. The writing will be terrible, self-conscious, I said to myself, shaking my smug head. At least I've got the sense to stick to novels. She was a wonderful poet, spare and breathing. I wondered why she would do what she was doing.

We all read from our work in progress in Banff. My poet colleague read a piece from her memoir. It remains for me the most powerful writing I have ever experienced. It was a piece about the city of Toronto, the map grid, and how the search for her sister's body proceeded along the gridlines. It left me breathless, like I had been punched.

When her book came out, my colleague sent me a copy. I had emailed her out of the blue to tell her what her reading had meant for me, how I'd been trying to write about my own experience but had struggled to find my voice. She sent me a quote from the American poet Louise Bogan. 'No woman should be shamefaced about giving back to the world, through her art, a portion of its lost heart.'

I do not know how my poet colleague managed interviews about her book. Her sister's death could bring tears to her eyes over lunch, could bring tears to all our eyes when she read from her work. When she sent me a copy of her book, I wrote her saying what I'd thought that day after lunch, how hopeless her project seemed to me, and that when I heard her read I knew how I'd misjudged her power, how her writing was a gift to the world.

I understand now my colleague's fear and compulsion. This happened, this was done, she was saying in her work. I must honour my sister, honour myself.

I sometimes wish my life had been another life, that I'd followed the trajectory that fierce ten-year-old girl at the pool was on. She might have looked at my teacher and her husband and screwed up her nose and laughed and run away. She might never have gone where I have been.

I wonder too what my teacher and her husband will make of this story, if it finds them. Will they see what harm we did, what harm they did, or will they be furious, call me on the phone and say, How dare you, after all we did for you? Or dress up in a rabbit suit and come and shoot me.

Fear

A YEAR AFTER DAVID AND I moved in together, although I didn't know it, my teacher and her husband came back to Brisbane from Melbourne to live. I'd had no contact with them. I hadn't told them I was seeing a counsellor. They hadn't met David. At least once before—after Katie Flannery's funeral—they turned up in my life and I'd gone back to them.

My teacher's husband rang my friend Louise and said, 'Let's surprise Mary-Rose,' and there they were at Louise's house when David and I arrived for lunch one Sunday.

Unless you've been through something like this, and I hope you haven't, you can't imagine how I felt when I saw my teacher and her husband at my friend Louise's house. For the first time, I was facing what transpired between us: that a married couple I trusted like parents betrayed that trust. I was dreaming of monsters almost every night. Louise was someone outside the circle of betrayal, who remained my friend through my darkest years.

I felt as if I was skinless.

I was terrified of my teacher's husband, terrified of both of them, the power they once had over me, the lack of self-regard I'd had in our relationship. I left soon after I arrived without saying anything to anyone about why. I walked out the door and David followed.

When I arrived home, I fell apart, called Mick. He made a time to see me the next morning. He said I was frightened because this was a violation of my boundaries. We'll draw a ring around you, he said. You'll be safe. I didn't feel safe, not for days. Louise had no idea what was wrong. I said I was sorry about ruining the lunch but I couldn't see my teacher and her husband anymore and I didn't want her to see them either. She went along with my request and didn't question me about it. I will always be grateful she did this.

The dreams became more frightening. It was weeks before my fear subsided. I was afraid my teacher and her husband would destroy me. They were bigger than Mick, although he was too stupid to know it, and they would overwhelm him and I would be trapped and they would destroy me for telling him what I had told him.

A few months after my teacher and her husband turn up at the surprise lunch, I find out my teacher's husband is studying on campus, because he starts leaving notes on my car.

Saw your little car. It's looking great. Regards.

How are you going? I'm back at tech. Best.

I ignore them. Work has helped me in these years, made me feel I can contribute something useful to the world. I love my job, the neatness of it, the way I can craft policy and make the world neater, more orderly, the high regard in which I am held at the institute—now a university, thanks to a submission I wrote. I am well paid. I work for important men and they are kind to me. They respect me and value my skills.

And then, one night when I am working back, my teacher's husband turns up in my office. It is late and I am frightened because I think I am the only person left in the building and I don't know what he will do. He walks in and sits down.

I realise he knows where I work, where my office is on the campus. I don't know how he knows this as it is not publicly available information.

My teacher's husband is sitting across from me and talking to me as if there is nothing wrong between us and yet I am starting to name the unnameable things that have happened.

He leans over and brushes a piece of lint from my jacket breast pocket and smiles and says, 'There, that's better.'

I am terrified. I talk to him as if this feels normal but I am terrified.

A face appears at the door. It is Brian, who is still in the corridor, working back, like me. Brian says, 'Excuse me,' to my teacher's husband, says to me he has a quick question, asks the question, which I answer.

Brian is still standing at the door, holding his glasses in his hand the way he does. He looks at me and then at my teacher's husband. He comes into my office and sits down. I introduce them.

They make small talk. My teacher's husband laughs loudly at Brian's jokes. They talk about the new building. My teacher's husband talks about the army and how well they do things. Brian nods and smiles. He fiddles with his glasses in his lap and then sucks the arm and watches my teacher's husband carefully.

Brian doesn't leave the room, despite the fact that he's asked me what he came to ask me and has run out of small talk. He sits there, his arms crossed, implacable, smiling.

Eventually, my teacher's husband takes his leave, shakes Brian's hand. 'See you round,' he says to me. I don't respond.

After he leaves, Brian says, 'You looked like you could use company. Who was that guy?'

'Someone I used to know.'

I do not wish to bring my teacher and her husband here where I have found a home.

'Are you sure you're okay?' Brian says then.

'Yes,' I say. 'Fine.'

'All right. See you tomorrow.'

⌇

After my teacher's husband turns up at my office, Mick suggests we get them in for a chat. 'They're not leaving you alone,' he says. 'Maybe this is a good opportunity for us to work with them.'

I can't believe he can be so casual. 'Don't you know what they're like?' I say.

He smiles, dictates a note to them to invite them to come to a therapy session to talk through what has happened between us. Surprising myself, I send the note.

It is my teacher who rings me, not her husband. She says they will not come to see my therapist. They don't like to dwell on negative things that are now long past, she says. They think it is time to get on with life. They hope I'll respect their confidence in the future as they've respected mine.

⌇

I write them a letter, with help from Mick, telling them goodbye. I say that while I accept that their approach is not to dwell on negative things, I am finding that the negative things are interfering with my ability to live my life. I say that working through negative things and getting free of them is my approach to life and that this is an important point where our approaches differ.

I say that keeping aspects of our relationship secret, including the sexual aspects, has been harmful, that while I have no wish to make them not okay, I will only respect their confidence to the extent it allows me to respect myself.

I say I do not want to have anything further to do with either of them.

When I finish the letter, Mick says he wants me to be sure I don't want any contact with my teacher and her husband in the future before I cut off all ties. He says it is a severe response and it might be useful for me to have some contact with them so that, over time, they become less gods or monsters and more just people.

I say I am very sure I don't want anything to do with them. I want to be free of them.

I say my final goodbye in that letter. It will be another two decades before I feel free of them.

～

I have seen my teacher's husband three times since then. The first time, he was coming out of the Village Twin Blue Cinema with a teenage girl. I told myself she was his niece and have hoped many times since that she was not another girl like me.

The second time he was in the city at Bar Merlo with two or three men. This was many years later and I couldn't believe how small he seemed. He was sitting down, so I had no point of comparison, but there's something about tall men, they take up space. He looked as if he'd shrunk in the intervening years but perhaps, after all, I had grown.

The men with him looked like middle-level managers in the council. He wasn't in a suit, it was a button-up shirt and slacks, and he looked like a middle-level manager too.

I watched him for a long time, unbeknownst to him. To me as a teenager, my teacher's husband was larger than life, superhuman, but there in the mall he seemed so ordinary, so unremarkable, neither Superman nor one of Superman's worthy opponents.

The third time I saw my teacher's husband was a few years ago. I was walking a mountain track with my friend Cass. He was with a group of men with black t-shirts. I was coming up the far slope when I passed them going the other way.

I waited at the top for Cass and the group of men passed me again, this time on their way back down. We were alone in the bush, me and these twenty black-shirted men. I wasn't sure it was him—I'm still not—but only because I wasn't afraid. I looked him in the eye and held his gaze until he looked away. And I wasn't afraid.

I saw my teacher too, twice, without her husband: once in the city at a crossing in Adelaide Street, and the second time at the Mt Coot-tha Planetarium with her daughter, who looked about thirteen. They seemed close.

I looked at my teacher but all I could see was the Russian doll I'd seen when she was first my teacher. Underneath that was nothing I understood.

I have a photograph of a ten-year-old girl. She is there by the pool. She dives in. The water is cold on her skin, the sounds of the world are softened, and she swims and swims and swims.

Writer Mary-Rose

THIS MAY NOT BE A true story. As a young journalist, my mother was lucky enough to meet the famous children's writer Enid Blyton, who stopped in Brisbane briefly. There was a press conference in a hangar out at the airport. Many important people were there—the Australian publisher, someone from the British High Commission, someone from the Australian prime minister's office, along with reporters from Sydney. My mother was representing her paper, *The Courier-Mail*. I have seen a photograph of her in those days, in a broadbrimmed cream hat with cream gloves and catwoman glasses, excited to be there with the other journalists.

Miss Blyton herself was surprisingly small, according to my mother, and dressed, as my mother would report faithfully in the next day's edition, in an aqua twinset, hat and pearls, looking just like the Queen Elizabeth. We see her there, awkward Miss Enid Blyton, shimmering across the Brisbane tarmac, entering the hot tin hangar, fans whirring, everyone looking her way.

The press conference started with an introduction from the Australian publisher and some words of welcome from the high commissioner. Miss Blyton was noticeable for her silence, my mother said, and then it was time for questions. Someone asked, 'Miss Blyton, where do you get the ideas for the Noddy stories?'

Miss Blyton cocked her head, looked at the questioner like he was a dog that had talked, opened her mouth, closed it, opened it again and said: 'Why, Noddy tells me, of course.'

In my family, this was a story about mad old Enid Blyton who believed in Noddy. But she was not mad, Enid Blyton, not at all, and now I think I know what she was talking about. In fact, if I were to give advice to a young writer, which I'd never presume to do, but if I did, I'd tell the young writer to listen to Noddy.

Gail Sher says writers write. It is one of her four noble truths about writing. I can never remember the other three. Writers write. It's often comforting, that notion, that all I need to do is push this pen across this page in enough predawn or candlelight so that I will be able to read it later if I decide I want to. Writers write, and sometimes when they write, they hear Noddy.

When I was a child, I was good at listening to Noddy, as children are. My brothers and I built Lincoln City in the dirt under our house. My oldest brother Ian was in charge. He'd build roads and infrastructure while Andrew, the brother closest to me, would fill the dam. I created stories for Lincoln City, mostly based on terrible events. I don't remember individual citizens and the effect of my events on them. Character is so much harder than plot, and growing up on Superman and Batman comics with their strong narrative pull, I was never much enamoured of stories that don't go anywhere.

Our stories often ended with a flood. 'The dam's busted! Run for your lives!' Andrew yelled, taking over whatever plot I was working up and ensuring the story wouldn't suffer from ennui. With his arm he'd grade the dirt that plugged the spillway on the dam. Our day's roads and buildings would be destroyed in the ensuing torrent.

Raymond Chandler used to say that whenever his stories got boring, he'd have a man walk in with a gun. Andrew was our man with the gun.

The next day, we'd rebuild Lincoln City.

⌇

I have loved stories for as long as I can remember. At rest time in kindergarten, with nothing else to do but stare at the ceiling for those nine hours after lunch, I amused myself with stories. My bed was often shifted to an isolated place because my chatter would keep other kids awake.

Later, I had teachers who saw in me a storytelling need and a strange connection with words. Miss Tyquin in year five gave me marvellous projects to do. Write an Aboriginal legend. How the budgerigar got its stripes. Mrs Thomson in year eight fed my creativity and also red-lined my purple prose. I remember when we had to rewrite the story of Beowulf and Grendel, she circled, *His bones snapped like a Cadbury Crunchie bar*, and wrote in red: *You could do better*. She recognised in me a love of words and stories and language, and she fed it with her own. I wrote poetry in later school years, mostly self-conscious and tortured but also innocent and beautiful. I wrote about my father, the rainforest, my feelings for my teacher.

When I became a cadet journalist, I couldn't believe I was going to be allowed to write stories all day and that this would be my job. I loved interviewing people, finding out what they thought and felt, what had happened to them, and writing about it. I loved playing with the words, working up a lead so that the reader would know everything they needed in that first paragraph. I loved the discipline that journalism demands, the economy I am no longer capable of.

⌒

After I came home from Melbourne, I stopped writing altogether. I had nothing to say and no connection to the spiritual place where writing must come from for me. I had no connection with myself at all.

It wasn't until my late twenties, after I met David, that I started writing again. What had been easy in childhood had become more difficult than I could ever have imagined. It took time. It took years. It is still a struggle.

To write, I discovered, you need to achieve egolessness, not easy when you have an ego the size of Mount Vesuvius. You need to be nothing but this moment and this pen scratching across this page. I cannot be thinking about how much I've lost, what a bad person I am, what a wonderful novel I am conjuring, what terrible things reviewers will write. I must be here, show up, bear witness, get out of the way. Writers write.

Angels

SOON AFTER MY TWENTY-EIGHTH BIRTHDAY, David and I bought an apartment. We painted the white walls white, bought a couch, a refrigerator. We talked about travelling. We travelled. We went to Rome. We got married at the Australian embassy in Paris and blew the money my father gave us as a wedding present on a spectacular lunch in a very fine Parisian restaurant. Mum and Dad had divorced by this time, and Mum had gone to live in Perth, where my brother Andrew had settled.

David let me be young, if that makes sense. He let me be. I was the happiest I'd been since I was a child. I left QUT to write full-time after my first novel, *No Safe Place*, was published. I was so sad to leave. I am terrible at goodbyes and, by then, I was Vice-Chancellor Dennis Gibson's executive officer. QUT had given me a safe haven, and Dennis became a dear friend. His ideas were so elegant. Sometimes I would read a draft he'd handwritten late at night, and on the other side of the paper I'd see a bunch of equations—he did maths to relax. Often, I wouldn't change a word of what he wrote. Every now and then it was poetry, although he had absolutely no awareness that it was.

I often think of Dennis when I meet people who tell me they cannot write. He was probably the last person I made into one of my heroes, and although he didn't know it, just by being an ordinary good man, he helped me to heal.

No Safe Place is a novel about a sexual misconduct case in a university. My second novel is a love story couched in a mystery called *Angels in the Architecture*. I don't know why I wrote such complicated plots in those days. Perhaps it was to hide that one sentence every novelist is supposed to hide in every novel. I piled plots on like mattresses in the hope the reader would and wouldn't feel the pea.

Angels in the Architecture is set in Brisbane and reflected the happiness I was experiencing in my life while I was writing. I was with David. I think I was always meant to be a happy person. I'd certainly rather be happy than normal now. In *Angels in the Architecture*, there is a dark secret, but it is a happy story, in which love redeems.

The site for *Angels in the Architecture* is a hill not unlike Duncan's Hill in Fortitude Valley in Brisbane—the site of

All Hallows'—and the university campus of the novel used to be a girls' school. The idea came to me when I attended my twenty-year reunion at All Hallows'. I had been messing about with an idea for a sequel to *No Safe Place*, had written two complete manuscripts, in fact, neither of which engaged me past about page three. I was starting to panic, having left a good job to be a writer and finding I had nothing worthwhile to write.

I was asked back to All Hallows' to speak to my peers on why I had been expelled (I was asked to leave, not expelled, I kept telling the organisers). I can't remember what I said, but I remember seeing the Story Bridge drawn in lights out the window of the concert hall where the reunion was held, seeing the statues and icons that populated the stairwells, smelling that wood polish they'd been using at All Hallows' when my grandmother was a girl, even seeing the bustling little nun who had been principal when I left, still bustling. It was suddenly so very precious. I wished I'd never left there.

When I was working on the manuscript, I rang All Hallows', at David's urging, to see if I could spend time on the site to mull. I was hesitant about ringing; they'd thrown me out, one way or another, and would not welcome me back. 'No one will even know who you are,' David said. 'They'll have forgotten.'

I was put through to the principal's office. I said my name. 'I remember you,' the principal's secretary said flatly. She'd been asked to mind our class when I was in year nine because her then boss, the deputy principal who was my class teacher, was called out urgently. The secretary had only been at the school a few weeks then. I don't remember what I did, and she didn't tell me. But my chances of being anonymous were destroyed. I didn't hold much hope of being offered a corner to work in.

To her credit, Sister Anne O'Farrell welcomed me back to the school and gave me a little room and desk to work on my manuscript. The school was much changed. There was a poster in the hall outside my room which read *Care, Share and Dare*. The students were bussed to a rally for reconciliation with Aboriginal and Torres Strait Islander people in King George Square. All Hallows' was the only school to attend. The girls I met wrote fantastic material in our workshops. I did not think they would banish each other to the sports field to hide.

At the launch of *Killing Superman*, my third novel, Sister Anne Hetherington, who was principal when I was thrown out of All Hallows', and Sister Anne O'Farrell, the principal who welcomed me back twenty years later, were both in attendance. I acknowledged them in my speech, adding that both had made good decisions.

I continued to work hard in those years. I worked on my writing like it was drill. David said my boss was the boss from hell, meaning me. My father's legacy, I suppose: good enough, almost good enough, never quite good enough.

I would say to people: I am not someone who has regrets. I am not someone who has regrets. I remember meeting up with my friend Kris Olsson, who was writing an article about adoption. Her mother lost a child. Complicated, she said, tragic. I gave up a baby, I told her. It's not the wrong decision for everyone. I felt angry with her, as if she was talking about things she couldn't possibly understand. I had made the right decision, I believed. What would she know? She nodded but I could see in her eyes she thought I was defensive. Later, much later, she reminded me I once said this, that it wasn't the wrong decision for everyone. I wondered who I was trying to convince.

I have that one letter from you, written when you were a girl. You told me the things you liked to do. You started by asking me why I gave you up. It was a fair question but I didn't give you a fair answer. I gave you the answer I'd been given. I wanted the best for you, a home with two parents who could provide for you. My motives were never as noble as that. I did what would keep my teacher and her husband happy. That's the truth. I didn't even think of you.

In my late twenties, I contacted my daughter's other mother through the adoption agency because I wanted to tell her who my daughter's father was. I wouldn't tell her all the truth, about what happened between my teacher and her husband and me. I was too deeply ashamed to tell anyone about that, too frightened of what would happen to me if I did tell. I kept the secret. All the same, making sure my daughter knew where she came from was important to me. It was a start.

I made contact through the agency. Jenny Fish had left by that time and I spoke with someone named Frankie who said there was a letter from my daughter's other mother on their file, written when my daughter was six. Now my daughter was a teenager. I gave Frankie my address so she could send me the letter. She told me that if I wanted to write back, all I needed to do was put a letter in an envelope and send it to Frankie and Frankie would forward it on.

I read that first letter from my daughter's other mother which told me about my daughter's life, what she liked to do—music and drama—but it was like she was a Martian talking about a Martian child. I don't know what I expected, but I had no idea why she was telling me these things, no idea of who this child was to me.

David and I went to Melbourne soon after this. We flew down for a long weekend. Before then, if I had to go to Melbourne for work, I told cab drivers to take a different route into the city so that we didn't go past the hospital. Sometimes I still saw Grattan Street, because Melbourne is such a perfect grid that all the streets cross one another somewhere.

David and I walked past the hospital where my daughter had been born. I didn't feel anything and it made me confident I'd got over whatever it was I had to get over. We walked past 101 Grattan Street, and that's when I found it didn't exist. We even went to the Catholic Family Welfare Bureau in Carlton, but I was too nervous to talk to anyone.

For a Girl

After I got home, I wrote a letter to my daughter's other mother. I told her as much of the truth as I could. I said my daughter's father was an officer in the army and was married when I met him. I said I didn't want to keep secrets.

My daughter's other mother wrote back. She said her husband was uncomfortable about contact with me. She would write once or twice a year but would not share their name and address. And she sent pictures: in the beginning, a little girl with a littler girl, also adopted, my daughter's younger sister, an adult cuddling both chopped off at the hips; another of the first girl, older or younger now, I wasn't sure, with freckles, on a camping trip in a tie-dye shirt.

Other pictures came too in the months that followed, a girl in a school uniform, a young teenager in a sweatshirt and jeans, an older teenager dressed for a school formal, older again with a boyfriend.

I stared and stared at those pictures. They were pictures of a person who didn't look like me, or maybe did, I couldn't tell. I stared and stared at them. I couldn't read them.

With her first letter, my daughter's other mother sent that letter from my daughter, the one asking me why I gave her up. It's still a good question.

In another letter, my daughter's other mother asked questions about the father, the officer in the army who was the father. I had sent a photograph of him. My daughter looked like him, her other mother said, had his winning smile. Did

I notice that? she said. Could I tell them more about him? My daughter was curious, her other mother said.

I did my best, but I was terrified of my teacher's husband at that time, for I had started to understand what great power he had wielded in my life, what that had meant for me. I told what truth I could, but I did not cope well with her questions. I didn't know what to say. I couldn't even tell myself the truth, let alone someone else.

⌣

After a year or so of writing to my daughter's other mother, I decided I should move on from that stage of my life. I ticked a box somewhere in my head. If I thought about the past from then on, it was a tiredness I felt, a fatigue that made every muscle of my body weigh heavily. I continued to slip into these dark moods I didn't understand. They were less debilitating—my first bout of therapy had left me functional, so I wasn't drinking the way I once was—but no less frightening. Mick had said that these were moments of regression when I became a helpless child, perhaps an infant, facing life, terrified. I wasn't so sure.

It's there in the first three novels, of course. *No Safe Place* is about sexual misconduct and betrayal. *Angels in the Architecture* is about trusting someone enough to love them. *Killing Superman* is about grief. They are not a trilogy, except in terms of how they tell the story I couldn't tell. You just have to join the dots.

Bridges

IN MY THIRTIES I DEVELOPED a fear of bridges. I first experienced this fear on the Golden Gate Bridge that spans San Francisco Bay where it meets the Pacific Ocean.

When I set out on foot at the Fort Point end of the bridge, I had no idea what was to come. As I became suspended by the bridge rather than the earth, the ground under my feet began to move, rather like when you stand too close to a lift shaft. Cars and trucks whizzed by at great speed on the left. The blue bay was moving far below on the right. The wind blew me this way then that. Quite suddenly, I became afraid.

The Golden Gate Bridge is one of the longest suspension bridges in the world. Along its length, I discovered, are cement pylons which have something to do with holding the bridge in place. They appeared very sure of themselves on that flimsy structure of wires and bolts. The pylons are large—I could not get my arms around them—and painted the same russet as the rest of the bridge. I don't know how many pylons there are on the bridge; I didn't count them.

What I did on the Golden Gate Bridge that day when my fear of bridges hit me for the first time was walk between those pylons, and at each pylon I stopped. I didn't care who was watching or what kind of ritual they thought I was enacting. As I walked, every muscle in my body was tense with fear. I stopped at each pylon and hugged it. The pylons were not quite safe, but they were heaven compared with the open bridge, which was less than air. I held each pylon until I felt I could go on.

My fear became more and more intense. My heart was pumping so loudly in my ears, my chest hurt. David read from a guidebook that the two main cables of the bridge each weigh 11,000 tons. They have 25,572 separate wires. Imagine if one unravelled, he said, trying to help with a joke. I did not laugh.

Afterwards, we told the story at dinner parties, him doing the walk, looking like the Tin Man, me describing the feeling. People wanted to know why I kept going. Some assumed I saw it as a way to conquer my fear, to show it for what it was, some memory of unsafety, but I had no such goal. Some thought me brave in a weird way. I am not brave.

It was simple. I am an optimist in my deepest heart and remain optimistic through much discouragement. I knew fear was behind me on the bridge. I'd felt it, each step leaden, my legs heavier and heavier, my arms and neck like planks, my head like a medicine ball on top of me. Behind me was fear—I knew that—and what lay in front must be better, I thought to myself. So rather than turning back to fear, I kept going.

The only way forward was through.

As it turned out, I was as terrified in the last steps of my walk—between the final pylon and the bridge's end—as I was at the first. More so, because fear has a way of manufacturing itself. And the fact I walked across the bridge and lived made me no less frightened when, later, I was driving across the Oakland Bridge, a feat of engineering you might marvel at. All I could do was watch the bumper of the car in front, my shoulders hunched over the wheel, convinced I was driving to oblivion.

At the other end of the Golden Gate Bridge is Sausalito, an ordinary town where I walked around as if I was a normal person.

I went home to Australia and conceived a child most people thought was my first child.

The only way forward was through.

Otis in the world

BETWEEN DAVID AND ME WAS the question of children. I asked myself the question and I never knew the answer. I wasn't sure why. David was ambivalent, he always said, but of course he'd go along if I wanted children; he just couldn't quite see himself as a father.

And then, at thirty-eight, I wanted a child. I just knew I did, as simple as that.

We tried for several years, doing the things you do, having sex, and when that didn't work as quickly as expected, undertaking research on the internet, adopting its many helpful suggestions. Having sex at special times of the day, the week, the month; rubbing cervical mucus between one's fingers to determine an ovulating consistency—egg white being the goal; changing the food I ate; changing the food David ate, the kind of underpants he wore—the looser the better to keep those poor little sperms cool—the position in which we lay with one another. It can become an obsession. It did.

And then I had an early miscarriage—a blighted ovum, it's called. Dr Tig, who'd been my doctor for twenty years and knew the truth about my earlier life before many people, rang to tell me the blood results. 'I'm sorry to say it's bad news,' she said in her lovely Dr Tig voice, 'but there's a silver lining. It means everything is working according to plan. So just keep trying.'

Fine, I thought. We'll keep trying.

No problem, David said.

The weekend after the blighted ovum was our tenth wedding anniversary. We didn't normally go to Coolangatta but that was where David had asked me to marry him so we decided to book a unit there.

I was out of sorts, tired beyond belief, a weight behind my heart, muscles aching. I didn't connect my mood with the miscarriage. I didn't even think about it. I had no idea the blighted ovum would raise any feelings at all in me. I never connected what had happened to me as a teenager with me as a middle-aged woman. I was in my head not my body where I had been since I was a teenager.

On the way down to the coast, I picked a fight with David about where we were staying. We bickered about the car I rented too. We bickered about bickering. I withdrew from David, went inside myself seeking safety. And then I fell apart.

I was alone in the apartment we'd rented. I'd told David to get out. I remember I was crying, coughing and choking. I couldn't get air into my lungs for a time. It was very frightening. My body was responding and I had no control.

It was late the same afternoon. David had come back and I had calmed down enough to let him hold me. I said I was sorry for yelling. I didn't know what was wrong. I had been so afraid. Now I wanted to leave Coolangatta. I needed to be somewhere else.

In the rental car we'd bickered over earlier—a sports car of sorts, a Volvo convertible, which was the opposite of a sports car, as David pointed out—we drove down to Byron Bay for the sunset.

It was like stepping outside after a storm, entering the world after all that emotion, for now everything was peaceful and charged with meaning and filled with beauty. Just for those hours, I was back in my body, back to myself and I felt at home. On the way back to Coolangatta, I had Neil Diamond's *Hot August Night* blaring through the Volvo stereo. Even David sang along. He is not normally a fan.

I thought we would be all right. I told David I was giving up on having a child. I stood on the beach and looked out through The Pass. I thought we would be all right.

For a Girl

⌒

We bought a new car, a small car. We bought our architect-designed clinker-brick townhouse in St Lucia that had so many child hazards you wouldn't in all conscience consider bringing children there, not even to visit—a mezzanine floor with a toddler climbable balustrade onto slate tile, stairs with no balustrade over the same slate tile, a veranda with low railings and a drop to paving.

I started a corporate-writing business to supplement my novel-writing income. University colleagues and then government clients started engaging me to write their reports. I discovered I loved researching an issue in as much depth as I could, listening to a single reviewer or group, and coming up with a report. It was intellectually challenging, interesting and great fun.

I started making money. We had a couple's car and a couple's house and a couple's income. I said I would get on with life without children. I didn't really feel too bad about it; I told myself I didn't. I thought I wasn't meant to have children. I think in truth I thought I wasn't good enough to have children.

And then I was pregnant.

⌒

We called him Otis from the start, from the time he was an unblighted ovum, not because we'd intended to name him Otis—we didn't even know his sex—and not because I was set on having a boy, but because I would not call the baby 'it' and as far as I knew Otis was a name a boy or girl might have. I had never met an Otis. I loved Otis Redding's version of the Sam Cooke song 'A Change is Gonna Come'. There were the elevators, and the dog and cat movie, but I didn't think of either of those. It wasn't as if we were going to name a child Otis. It was just a name for now.

We had bought a Judy Watson etching called *Visceral Memory* that year. I loved its strength, soft black lines on an ochre background around a core of life. Much later I read that Watson had painted her spine series, including *Visceral Memory*, when she was heavily pregnant with her son Otis. I later met the artist and told her how we'd come to her work and that our son was named Otis too. What are the chances? we both said.

Visceral Memory was on our bedroom wall when Otis was conceived. It's on our bedroom wall still.

⌒

I didn't know the writer Kim Wilkins well, but we read together at a writers' cabaret early in my pregnancy, and I thought she was immensely clever and funny. After the panel, we were talking and realised we would both be on Mount Tamborine, south of Brisbane, one weekend soon. I was house-minding and she and her partner—musician Mirko Ruckels—were visiting friends, so we had lunch together. Kim and Mirko talked about wearing their earth suits. David and I used to say, 'Imagine the moon.' We knew we would be friends.

Somehow, although neither of us was supposed to tell anyone we were pregnant, waiting the sixteen weeks, we both stumbled out with it that day on Mount Tamborine. I was further along, almost sixteen weeks. Kim's baby would be born two months after Otis.

Like almost everyone in my life, I hadn't told Kim I'd already had a baby, and by the time I was ready to tell her, it was too late. For me, it was a blessing. Kim would be the friend I could be a first-time mother with, could be unsure with, could feel I had a right to be a first-time mother with. I knew it wasn't honest, but I didn't know how to tell her the truth, not then.

⟋⟍

I was heavily pregnant in the turning of summer into fall, surely the most beautiful few months on the planet. The light is soft, the days short and the air crisp. I remember watching small things in the garden of our townhouse—light on rocks, a baby turkey, a lemon tree next door—and feeling that I was part of everything.

⟋⟍

I remember the first night with Otis in the world as if it was yesterday. Louise and Gerard had been up to visit and they had left, and then David left. I was alone with Otis, exhausted and euphoric.

There was a woman in the bed next to me, yet to be delivered of her twins, and she was snoring sporadically and unpeacefully, like a plane taking off. It woke Otis, who woke me with his cry. I had no idea what to do and a kindly midwife came and changed his nappy and put him into bed facing me and left us.

For the rest of the night, we stared at one another in the strange light of a night-time hospital while the woman snored. I looked into his face and had the only glimmer in my life of understanding God. I looked into his face and he looked into mine and I was thinking about him having been inside me not a few hours before and now he was this whole little person in the world. And he was thinking about nothing, just staring at me, just being. I don't imagine I'll ever fully appreciate that moment.

⌐⌐

We would name him Otis after all. He had a mullet of dark red hair, a cone head on one side from his trip through the birth canal and a lightning strike birthmark between his eyes. We couldn't give him an ordinary name. He was not an ordinary child, although I suppose there's no such thing as an ordinary child.

⌐⌐

When I was in labour, I'd been unable to accept that I was going to give birth to a baby any time soon. My main midwife,

Maureen, who called me Mary-Rose and not an elderly primip, wanted me to get up on the bed so she could do an internal examination to see how far along I was. At first, I wouldn't do it.

We had only just arrived at the hospital. I had stayed at home as long as I could, the hospital being a place where I knew I wouldn't feel safe, even if I didn't know why. Finally, with both Maureen and Louise coaxing, I got up on the bed and Maureen did the examination and said, 'You're at ten centimetres,' which meant I was ready to give birth.

'Rubbish,' I said. 'You're just trying to make me feel better.'

When the obstetrician arrived, I told her what was going to happen. 'Barbara,' I said, 'we haven't met but let me tell you how it's going to be. We won't be doing an epidural. And we won't be having a caesarean.'

'You're about to have your baby,' Barbara said. 'There's no time for any of that. I'm just going to rupture your membranes.'

'Don't do that,' I said in a panic. 'It will speed up the labour.'

'The membranes are the only thing holding the baby in,' she said, exasperated at my failure to grasp the simplicity of the situation. 'Birth is imminent.'

Otis was born just a few minutes after that. He was lifted up onto my chest, where he stayed for the next hour because nobody had a mind to take him away.

I tell this as a funny story, the story of my labour with Otis, that here I was about to give birth but still not quite sure I was in labour. I tell it as a funny story. But it's not so funny really.

If my body betrayed me during my labour with Otis, if it lied about what was happening, who could blame it? My body knew, as none of the rest did—not Dr Barbara, not Maureen, not Louise or David, or even me in my mind. My body knew, as no one else knew, that to go on to that place of birth was the most dangerous thing; that birth is where the real pain begins.

⟋⟍

Our old townhouse belongs to friends who have their own baby now. When I visit I remember everything. It's as if my whole body is loose and warm and free again, surely for the first time since baby Ruth was born. A family of butcher-birds raised their young in a tree in our bushland park two, perhaps three years running while were there. We fed them from our veranda, to the chagrin of our greener neighbours. When Otis was tiny, those nightjars, mother and baby, sat in the tree outside his window. They made him safe, I believed, although I've since learned that nightjars and owls are dumb not wise—that's just PR—and could not keep a child safe.

Otis brought baby Ruth back to me, in his way, made me know finally what I'd lost when I handed my child to strangers, what I could never ever get back, and the act for which I cannot atone, the life I must let go of in order to live the life that's now mine.

PART III

Returning

Homeless

DAVID AND I HAD ALWAYS lived on terraces with trees. The hot brick unit we rented in Bellevue Terrace had a big old gum waving in the bedroom windows, promising breezes. We bought our first apartment in Stanley Terrace because it overlooked a giant fig in the park below. We traded up to our Prospect Terrace townhouse with its child hazards because it overlooked a bushland park.

When Otis came along, we made our townhouse as safe as we could. We had an architect design a retro-balustrade for the open staircase. We put shutters on the mezzanine and fixed a lockable screen to the door leading to the veranda with its low railing onto pavement.

But in the months after I hurt Otis with the stroller clip, I started to think we should move. It began as a vague notion and, over time, it became increasingly important. My body, which I'd always been able to rely on to do what it was told, set out on its own, reclaiming its right to have a say in things.

I would find myself on the floor like the first time, shaking and crying uncontrollably, with no idea what had set me off or what would calm me. I never knew when it would happen, where it came from, or when it would end. It frightened me.

I hadn't felt at home in my body for years, although I also hadn't been aware of that fact. Suddenly, now, I knew I wasn't at home in my body and it was terrifying.

I started to believe that if we moved we would be all right. We were a family. A boy needed a yard and dirt. We should find a real house, a proper home, and I would be all right.

⌒

We searched for a house in a terrace. We searched the internet and then, on weekends, we spent hours walking through other people's houses, finding out what books they read. I decided I wanted an old house because Louise had an old house. Old houses don't have the poisons of new houses, the formaldehyde and other chemicals that leach out of new building materials, I said to David. Otis will be safe in an old house. There will be other children, and every weekend we'll wear old business shirts as smocks and paint each other's noses while we laugh uncontrollably at what fun we're having.

David was not so sure.

After a year of searching, Brisbane was at the top of a boom and houses were even more expensive than when we started. Our townhouse had sold and we didn't have enough money to buy a house in the areas where we were looking, let alone one in a terrace with trees. The houses we looked through were not flash or well-to-do, just inner-city. Inner-city had become the place to be, the real estate agents told me. Traffic, they said. People are giving up their outlying mansions so they don't have to sit in traffic.

⌒

When I was pregnant with Otis, I'd been to see a woman named Stace who did pregnancy massage in the kahuna style, a Hawaiian treatment based on movement and breath. I thought it would help me to get ready for labour. After Otis was born, I stopped seeing Stace, but in the week after I hurt him with the stroller clip, she contacted me, out of the blue, to say she had moved. She wanted to give me her new number, her message said.

I have always been a cynic when it comes to spirituality, both the traditional kind that incorporates incense and the sacred host, those small circles of dry bread that stuck to the roof of my mouth in childhood, and the new age kind that leads all sorts of practitioners to tell me the most outrageous things about my irises, auras and past lives. I am the daughter of two journalists. My father schooled me in scepticism. I can laugh with anyone who cares to about crazy therapies. My jokes will probably be funnier than theirs.

I was this cynic until I hurt Otis with the stroller clip and then I was willing to do anything to get my life back. I was not a woman who was running with the wolves. I was limping through life, hoping no one would notice.

Stace broke her back in her life as a circus performer, recovered and studied bodywork. Before I saw her, I'd been deaf to my body, or my body had been mute.

I learned slowly. This is one of the things I learned: if your body needs to cry or make noise or punch the air or roll up in a ball and shiver, and instead you accommodate a small child—watch *Play School*, read stories, go for a little walk—or otherwise ignore what your body is telling you, your body will not stop trying to tell you. It will make you tired, more tired than you have ever felt. The weight will press down on you all day and into the night. It will make you unreasonable, like a bomb about to go off. The bomb will go off.

In our sessions, while Stace moved over my body, soothing, untying the knots, testing, breathing and singing, I often did nothing but cry. I howled out loud sometimes, tears springing from my eyes, snot falling from my nose to the floor, then shed quieter, saltier tears that brought a measure of relief.

At these times, I was nothing but the water of my tears, a long river. I had no idea I had so much crying in me.

Stace had Dr Seuss's fox in sox tattooed on her arm. I'd see it sometimes as she worked. Her dog Bea, who used to lie on the floor of the massage room, died in the time we were meeting. She got Bea's pawmark tattooed on her foot and I used to look at that too, through the hole in the massage table.

I learned that my body's pain often had a message. I started to talk to my body, to my right leg, to my back muscles, to my heart. Tell me, I would say, tell me what the matter is. And my body would speak. It may be that other forms of grief are locked somewhere else in us, but babies are in our bodies. They form there, they emerge from there, they remain connected there our whole lives. It was my body that needed to tell me, to help me learn what I had done.

Although I didn't know it at first, I had gone into the past to find baby Ruth, the child I gave to strangers. I would come back changed. It would take three years.

The house of my addled mind

WE BOUGHT THE HOUSE IN Thomas Street by accident. A real estate agent I'd come to know phoned to tell me she had this house that needed work and the price had come down. We went to see the house and ruled it out because it needed so much work and we didn't have enough money. Six months later, the price came down again and the agent phoned me and said we should make an offer. Although we didn't know it, she only included us in the invitation so she could push a buyer with more money than us up in price, but the other buyer withdrew at the last minute. The family who owned the house were keen to sell so they sold to us.

We bought the house by accident but, even so, everyone said we bought well. We got a survey map from olden times and found out Thomas Street was once called Enoggera Terrace. This seemed apt. There were no trees in the yard so we planted some.

The drought started.

Before the contract settled, we discovered the house itself had problems too. According to the surveyor, the western edge was sitting in the neighbour's yard. The solution, shifting the house, would be expensive and complicated. We could have backed out at that stage—our solicitor advised us we should—but we decided instead to proceed, not really knowing why.

The day we settled we went over and drank champagne. I hadn't been to the house since we'd bought it and even though it was empty of the detritus of a family's fifty years, it felt strangely cloying, as if one couldn't take in enough air. We quickly gravitated to the backyard. We returned a few days later with the architect and builder, and the same thing happened. We walked through the house and met in the yard. It's a strange thing to say, but it was as if the house pushed you out.

'Look at that view,' visitors said, and it buoyed me up.

At first we decided to renovate before we moved in, but then our rental sold so I suggested we should live in the house while we planned. This will be great, I told David, like camping. We'll understand the breezeways, the play of light at different times of day. It will make for a better renovation.

Before we moved in, we arranged for the men who wear special suits to remove the asbestos sheets that lined the kitchen and laundry. After they finished, our builder Dave found live termites in the back half of the house. The termites had eaten out most of the western wall, which we'd have to replace when we removed the aluminium cladding. Termites don't like hardwood, the termite exterminator told us, so the structure was probably okay. He was strangely enthusiastic. He described the termites' achievements like they were his children making the honour roll.

During the Christmas break, we went to the house intending to remove the wallpaper from the living and dining rooms and clean the mouldy ceilings. We'd already taken up the carpets after they filled the vacuum cleaner four times and were still nowhere near clean. We were to move in at New Year. Where the men in special suits had removed the asbestos sheets, Dave had put up plasterboard as a temporary fix. Our light switches hung out of the walls on bits of taped-up wire.

We used an abrading tool to score the wallpaper in the dining room, planning to steam it off so we could paint. I let Otis use the abrading tool, like a pizza wheel with spikes, as this was something he could do. Late on the first evening, I asked David why the wallpaper colour looked powdery, like lead paint looks powdery. We tested and found out that the wallpaper was full of lead. Lead was used in wallpaper dyes as well as paint, apparently, although most people don't know that. We had been letting Otis help all day. There were flakes of leaded paper everywhere.

We stopped immediately, removed Otis from the house and then cleaned the floors and masked as much as we could of the remaining leaded surfaces with paint or tape.

We researched lead poisoning. Children take up heavy metals at twice the rate of adults. A piece of lead paint the size of a ten-cent piece would kill Otis. Smaller amounts would affect his growth and brain development. In the United States, lead has been named the number one environmental hazard for children. We agonised over whether to get Otis tested, decided against it as the pain of a blood test seemed unfair and there was nothing we could do if we had poisoned him but wait.

Life-threatening acute lead poisoning is treated with chelating agents, chemicals that bind with the molecules of lead and take them out of the body. Chelating agents are themselves hazardous to human health. Sometimes they damage the liver or kidneys on their way through the body. But if the alternative is death, chelating agents are better than nothing. For chronic lead poisoning, chelating agents are not used. They're too dangerous. The only thing you can do is wait and hope. We masked and re-masked whatever leaded surfaces we came across and prepared to move in as planned at New Year.

When we started packing up to move, I realised I didn't want to bring my father's ashes with us to our new house.

Dad had died five years before. His ashes had followed me from Stanley Terrace, where he was in the laundry tub cupboard and couldn't see the fig tree, to Prospect Terrace, where he took up the back of the garage and missed the view of the gum tree in the bushland reserve, to the rented house that had nothing more than a backyard shed for him, though with louvres through which an edge of a mango tree was visible. I wasn't proud of the way I'd kept him, but I hadn't known what to do with him.

I had the ashes because the woman Dad had been living with when he died, Pat, offered them to us once Dad was cremated. My brothers had no interest. Mum was still in Perth. So I'd taken them.

Ian and I met Pat and her daughter for the first time at the funeral home where the consultant (that's what it said on her badge)—who had amazing fairy-floss-pink hair in a beehive—took us through possible coffin accessories. Pat and her daughter, the mother of a toddler, wanted to put a teddy bear on the coffin because, they said, Dugald so loved teddy bears. He regularly gave them to the toddler. Pat and her daughter wanted a teddy bear rather than a cross.

Pretending I was not, as a middle-aged woman, narcissistically wounded by my father's affection for this unknown toddler—the affection he had never shown me, his actual daughter—I began to wonder if we were in the right meeting.

I know denial is a natural phase of grief, but the Dugald Ian and I knew did not love teddy bears. He eschewed sentimentality of any kind. He told us Santa Claus was made up and thought 'Don't Think Twice, It's All Right' was a love song. His most frequent morning greeting was, 'You kids, shut up!' delivered in a considerable state of irritation because we'd made enough noise to disturb his sleep.

In the last decade of his life, Dad hadn't responded when I called and left messages. He'd lost touch with Mum as well, after he'd asked her to marry him again and she'd refused him (pride, you have to have some pride, she told me). I later learned he'd written near the end to tell her he was dying—metastatic brain cancer by the time they found it—and she'd spoken to him several times, but then he'd stopped calling. He'd also told her she wasn't to tell us he was dying, so she didn't.

⌒

I had a notion that if I could put my father to rest with his own mother, who had loved him dearly, I might find some peace about his death. By telephone, I confirmed that my grandmother's ashes were in a box in a wall at the crematorium gardens at Albany Creek north of Brisbane.

The next day, I put my father in the car beside me and drove out to the crematorium. I took Otis with me, explaining on the way the best I could the difference between cremation and burial, hoping that when we got there he wouldn't ask where the furnace was, hoping he would fall into a much-needed sleep on the way home. When we arrived, I left my father's ashes in the car and went inside with Otis. I didn't have an appointment.

I had told Susan, the consultant I'd spoken to on the phone, that I was seeking to lay my father to rest with his mother. We found two adjacent niches overlooking the garden.

'This will do,' I said. 'This will be perfect.'

'It will cost you to move your grandmother,' Susan said. 'And you'll need authority.'

'Yes, of course,' I said.

'And time,' she said. 'It will take time.'

There's no nice way to dump your father's ashes. While Susan answered a call, I took Otis and went out to the hot car and picked up Dad, whose sealed plastic urn was still in the Body Shop paper bag I'd carried it through three houses in. I took Dad and left him on Susan's desk and made an exit while she was still on the phone. Urgent, I mouthed. We're moving.

She stared at me as I backed out of her office.

Having done nothing for years, I found myself needing to deal with my father's remains *now*. I was becoming used to this new self that needed to do things now. It was as if my body was running the show for the first time in years, and I had as much choice as a newborn baby and no loud squeal with which to protest.

A few days later, I received a receipt for my father's ashes from Susan, together with a quote and many forms that needed many signatures.

⌒

We moved in after New Year as planned. I tried to create a home at Thomas Street but I didn't have enough energy to contend with a house that disagreed so vehemently. Come a cold snap in April, we discovered rats. I found evidence of them, a half-chewed apple, and then I started to hear them gnawing the wood inside the cupboards in the night. They are habitual gnawers, apparently, to keep their teeth a length that suits them.

Our rats lived in the roof cavity and came down in the night through the places where there were still no walls and ceilings, the front veranda, the lean-to laundry and toilet out the back. I was seeing a counsellor at the time, and he told me that rats will attack small children. He had a rat phobia, I learned, but for a few weeks, until we dealt with the rats, I slept in Otis's bed with him.

We set traps, baited with bread and peanut butter sprinkled with chocolate, all organic. I'd hear the traps snap in the night but the rats didn't die; they thumped around the kitchen with the traps on their backs. David had to go out and use a shovel to send them on to the next life. Finally, I bought poison, something I thought I would never do, and threw it into the ceiling cavity. The rats stopped coming.

I called the men in special suits to come back. Otis had found so many pieces of asbestos in the backyard that I could build a wall with it, I told them. I said the terminal diseases caused by asbestos—mesothelioma and lung cancer—take thirty years to manifest themselves and that while for David and me it was less important, for Otis it was a huge burden. He is three, I said. He will die a young man if you don't find all the asbestos. They stared at me and didn't say anything.

It was June and the house was a refrigerator. There were holes in the walls, in the floor, and no insulation in the roof. I was swimming at South Bank in unheated water. It was so cold I would shiver uncontrollably after I got out. In those months of midwinter, my swimming was something akin to ice bath treatment in a nineteenth-century Scottish mental hospital. When I was this cold, I forgot what I was upset about.

Otis was happy, oblivious to the dangers and relieved he was able to draw on the walls to his heart's content since they were coming down in the renovation, but I feared for David. He became more inward-looking. I think he worried about money, about how we'd afford the house if my life disintegrated any further. I was still meeting my work commitments but only barely. Someone told us that many renovations end in divorce. The architect did drawing after drawing but none of them worked.

For a Girl

Some mornings I arrived home from the ride into South Bank to swim and as I climbed the stairs to the front door felt heavier with each step until I reached the threshold. I wanted neither to go nor stay, just to remain there forever in the morning sun. It was the strangest feeling. I started to believe it had to do with the physical house as well as the house of my addled mind.

The sewer in Hope Street

ONE NIGHT AFTER DINNER, WE decided to go for a walk. Otis had an enduring interest in underground drainage systems. The year before we'd carried a small chisel-like tool and a torch with us on walks to lever the lids off water drains so we could have a good look at them. In the evenings at Thomas Street, we sometimes walked to an enormous water pipe in Hope Street and debated what kind of drainage system it was part of.

But this night, Otis had been slow putting his shoes on, slow getting ready, and it was like a weight bearing down on me, a weight that had been pressing me down all day. We had finally set out when Otis remembered he needed his builder's helmet. We must go back, he said. David said he would go back.

I yelled at Otis that I would not wait any longer, yelled at David, walked off flooded with feelings I could hardly contain.

I found a place to hide up the street, an open garage attached to a house whose residents I was sure were away. I crouched in a corner and made myself as small as I could. I was shaking as if cold and crying. Fear, I knew this to be fear now, although I didn't know what I was afraid of.

Some time later, David and Otis passed me, David chatting to Otis, trying to give the impression that we were a normal family.

I was still crying, holding on to a concrete wall. It was holding on to me. I watched David and Otis pass, a happy boy and his dad, and for the first time the thought occurred to me that they would be better off without me. They would be better off without me, and I would be able to end these tears.

I did not let this thought take hold, not then. I made myself walk after Otis and David. I found them where I knew I would find them, in Hope Street at the water drain. Is it a water drain? Or a sewer? I think it's a sewer. Yes, certainly a sewer. They were sitting up there and they saw me coming from the bottom of the hill and when I reached them David said my timing was perfect. Otis had just started to worry—had just started crying, in fact, I could see, because his mother had walked off in a blind fury for no reason he understood.

I let David hold me and I held Otis and the three of us sat there and in this way we survived.

~

As well as Stace, during our years at Thomas Street I was seeing a counsellor who practised solution-focused brief therapy. I'd gone to see Wayne when my first novel was published and I was getting ready to leave my salaried job and become a writer. Once I left work and was happily writing, I stopped seeing him. After I hurt Otis with the stroller clip, I went back.

Wayne was different from Mick, whose approach mixed family therapy with transactional analysis. If Mick was too complicated, Wayne was so simple I sometimes wondered if he understood anything. He certainly didn't look to my childhood to explain what was wrong. As far as I know, solution-focused brief therapy points us towards what we do right rather than what we do wrong and encourages us to do more of that.

Over two walls of his office, Wayne had put up drawings done by children he'd helped, and he had a climbing plant that he stuck to the wall so that it ran around the drawings. I went to see him fortnightly then weekly, and in the time we met, he covered a third wall. We talked for an hour at a time. At some stage, I told him that his therapy put a whole new meaning on the notion of brief. He smiled and said it was as brief as it could be.

For a Girl

He said things like: You need to see this in a context of what you are moving through. This is the hardest thing you have ever faced. You did the only thing you could in the circumstances. Sometimes you focus on what's wrong and not what's right. Here is your ego; here is your spirit. Breathe. He had very light blue eyes, or grey, that were among the kindest I've ever encountered.

I read Anne Manne on being a mother. She says you hand in your ticket to suicide at the door to motherhood. I reassured myself with this notion, that I had handed in my ticket at the door. But of course, once you have seen that place where pain might cease, you will go back, you will go back there and some will stay.

At the times I thought like this, I made myself look at a photograph of Otis and me. It's one David took on a trip to Byron the year after I had pinched Otis in the stroller clip. It's late afternoon. The sun has set and the sky behind us is extraordinary colours. Otis and I are in silhouette so you can only see our outline. We stand the same way and we're hand in hand against this beautiful backdrop. Even though you can't see our faces, you know we are close, at one in whatever we are doing, absorbed by what we are seeing, in the moment together.

The worst times were when I failed Otis, sometimes as a result of what I was coming to terms with, sometimes just because I fail as a mother, as mothers do. For me these failures became much larger. They confirmed that I was a bad mother, the worst mother you could be. I was the mother who gave her child to strangers. That was who I was.

I became stuck in a cycle of self-hatred: feelings in my body that I didn't recognise or respond to, Otis being a young child, losing my temper, deciding I was a bad mother, he would be better off without me. It was a cycle that could end nowhere but my death.

Wayne said two things that will remain with me my whole life. He said he believed many people had something to answer for in what happened to me but I was not among them.

And when—after I told him I was not getting better, I had thought of dying lately, I had planned it and worked up my plan—I asked him, 'Are you the person who can help me?', he gave me two names, one a psychiatrist who could medicate me, the other a psychologist who worked with adoptees.

He asked how I felt when he suggested those names.

I told him I was too tired to start with someone new.

He said, 'In that case, you are stuck with me. You are stuck with me until you are not so tired, and when you are not so tired you can go to see someone else if you think it will help, I will find someone, but for now, you are stuck with me.'

And what I will remember about this is that he did not give me the other option, the light-filled room, and I left him knowing I would be back.

Care

To: adoption@melb.centacare.org.au
Subject: Adoption
Date: 16 January

Hello, I gave up a daughter for adoption in Melbourne through the Catholic Family Welfare Bureau. Can you tell me who I might contact for information about my daughter? Thank you. Mary-Rose MacColl

---

To: maryrose@email.email
Subject: Adoption
Date: 17 January

Hi Mary-Rose,
I will send you a registration form so you can register for information about your daughter. There is a fee for service

set by the Department of Human Services, which is $75, or $30 for Health Care Card holders. Please return the form together with payment for us to begin the process. You are entitled to all information pertaining to you and non-identifying information regarding your daughter. If you wish to search for her, we will assist you with that. If you have any questions, please do not hesitate to contact me.
Regards,
Helen Administration

To: adoption@melb.centacare.org.au
Subject: Adoption
Date: 17 January

Hi Helen,
Thanks for responding so quickly. I had some contact with my daughter and her other mother some years ago but all the details are currently in storage and difficult to access quickly. I may wish to search for my daughter and will contact you once I've filled out the forms for information.
Mary-Rose

To: maryrose@email.email
Subject: Adoption
Date: 22 February

Hi Mary-Rose,
I should have clarified with you earlier whether you wanted the records you received previously reissued. As you are already registered, we should not have charged you the $75 registration fee, and I will arrange a refund for you. If

you want the records reissued (there is a $30 reissue fee), I will arrange a $45 refund, otherwise we will refund the full amount. Your case has been reopened, and a social worker will be in touch with you soon. Sorry for the delay.
Regards,
Helen Administration

To: adoption@melb.centacare.org.au
Subject: Adoption
Date: 22 February

Hi Helen,
Yes, it would be good if you could reissue whatever I have already, thanks.
Cheers,
Mary-Rose

To: adoption@melb.centacare.org.au
Subject: Adoption
Date: 27 March

Hi Helen,
I'm emailing again as I haven't received the records I requested from your office. Also, I sent a letter to my birth daughter's mother via you a couple of weeks ago and I wanted to make sure it has been forwarded on. Can you let me know when I might get copies of the records I requested, please? Thank you.
Mary-Rose

To: maryrose@email.email
Subject: Adoption
Date: 28 March

Hi Mary-Rose,
I am not sure if you have spoken to Katrina (your social worker) yet, but she is the one who will be sending everything on to you and forwarding the package. She will be in the office tomorrow, so I will ask her to give you a call. I am not sure what the delay is, but everything should be sent to you shortly.
Kind regards,
Helen Administration

To: adoption@melb.centacare.org.au
Subject: Adoption
Date: 28 March

Hi Helen,
No, I have not spoken to Katrina. I have not heard from anyone since your last email in February. Will Katrina know whether the letter I sent to my daughter's other mother a couple of weeks ago was forwarded on? I addressed it via you at Centacare. Thank you.
Mary-Rose

To: maryrose@email.email
Subject: Adoption
Date: 28 March

Hi Mary-Rose,
We have received your package for your daughter's mother and Katrina will be sending it on. I will ask her to give you a

call tomorrow so she can discuss things with you. Now that you have been allocated a social worker I don't really know what stage in the process it is up to. The records that you are entitled to have been copied and court records obtained, so I am sure Katrina would have been contacting you soon. I am sorry for the delay.

Regards,

Helen Administration

To: maryrose@email.email

Subject: Adoption

Date: 29 March

Hi Mary-Rose,

I'm sorry. I told you Katrina would contact you today, but she is at a workshop all day. I have spoken to her, and she will contact you next Tuesday (she only works part-time). I am sorry for the delay.

Regards,

Helen Administration

To: adoption@melb.centacare.org.au

Subject: Adoption

Date: 4 April

Dear Helen,

I am sorry to have to email you again but I have no other contact in Centacare. I am still to hear from anyone about:

- the records you have about my experiences of giving up a baby which I requested in January of this year;

- the letter I sent via you, by Express Post, to my birth daughter's mother a few weeks ago.

I know you and your staff are probably busy. I have been through a long and emotionally racking process for the last year or so. I had not anticipated that the agency would delay its response to me. It is a thorough blow. I really need to know that the letter to my daughter's other mother has at least been forwarded. I am asking you again to respond. I would prefer contact by email as most weekdays I have a young child who doesn't necessarily understand my need for focused telephone conversations. Thank you in advance. Mary-Rose

---

To: maryrose@email.email
Subject: Adoption
Date: 4 April

Dear Mary-Rose,
Katrina has sent a letter to you today. She is not in the office this afternoon and I am on leave for the rest of the week, so I can't check with her, but she has sent you a cheque for $45 (the amount overpaid for your records to be reissued) and I believe a copy of your records has been enclosed. Unfortunately, I don't know if the parcel has been sent on as yet. All mail that is exchanged through us must be checked before being forwarded, and as Katrina is out, I can't check that for you. I will be back at work again next Tuesday, so if you what you receive from Katrina is not satisfactory, please let me know and I will ask Katrina to contact you as soon as possible. I am sorry for the delay and hope that the correspondence from Katrina will cover your queries. Regards,
Helen

For a Girl

After I started seeing Wayne again, I began to want to know what happened to me when I was a teenager. I remembered only small moments of kindness and unkindness and there must have been more than these, great swathes of ordinary time that were simply gone. I wanted to know the truth.

We were still living at Thomas Street, still working on renovation plans. I was learning to let my body do its work. I read articles and books about post-traumatic stress disorder and much of it resonated. But the things I needed to do according to the books—cry or rage or otherwise express powerful feelings—weren't always easy to achieve. I had to look after a small child and meet work deadlines. I don't like strong emotions as a general rule. What I needed was a tap that would help me get into my body on demand. I found one. It is a song called 'The Long Road' sung by Eddie Vedder and Nusrat Fateh Ali Khan.

Once I found this song, I was able to go out on my bike early in the morning and cry my way to South Bank and swim in the lake there and then sometimes cry my way home. Some days I wouldn't need to cry but most days I did. For a while, I did this every morning, like exercise.

The words of the song were important but just as important was the sound of Nusrat's Qawwali chanting. It is hauntingly beautiful. For me, it was how I imagined grief might sound.

I yelled along sometimes as I rode. I wept. In real time, it didn't feel so easy. In real time, I worried I'd never get better. I trusted the process not because I had a plan. I trusted the process because I didn't have a choice. I'd have to say now that I was dragged kicking and screaming into trusting the process, frankly. If it hadn't been for Stace and Wayne, I may not have survived.

Other people on the bikeway saw me. I'm sure they thought I'd crossed the bridge from sanity and perhaps I had. These were the best days, when I could get to the yelling and the tears early in the morning. The worst days were before I knew what needed to emerge from me, when I would simmer and rage and have no idea why.

I could still be overwhelmed with feelings and I won't say they didn't frighten me. Of course they did. It was a kind of madness. I wondered what was happening. I wondered if I'd ever feel better. I drank, ate strong chocolate, survived as best I could. I learned that sometimes I had to settle Otis at something and go and get in the shower and let the tears come. Frankly, the greatest harm I did, to Otis, to David, was when I didn't get to the tears.

~

I decided to resume contact with my daughter's other mother, having written nothing since *Angels in the Architecture* was published. If I'd told myself anything, it was that I had 'worked through' the adoption. I'd moved on, I would have said. When Otis came along, I was hesitant to write for other reasons. I hardly knew what to say to her, to my daughter, now in her late twenties; that here I was, the young woman who gave a child to strangers, now a woman who has had another child she is keeping.

I sent a parcel to my daughter's other mother via the adoption agency. In it was a letter and a book that included an essay I wrote about birth. It was from a collection published by the State Library of Queensland, and a canny editor had encouraged me to write more personally. So I mentioned my first birth, my secret baby.

I put my letter and the book in a sealed envelope, as that was what I'd done in the past. A month later, I contacted Centacare by telephone for the first time. I spoke to Helen, who put me through to social worker Katrina.

⌒

Katrina worked on Mondays and Wednesdays. She told me she was a custodian. She said it twice. Katrina hadn't had time to photocopy the records but she would, she said. She hadn't forwarded the letter yet, she said, because she was checking that the address was current.

She'd had the letter for over a month and now she was checking that the address was current. I let this go. I knew I was not an easy person at that time.

A day later, Katrina emailed to tell me my daughter's other mother had rung her to say yes, she wanted the letter. Katrina said she'd forwarded the letter and book. It hit me when I read her email. She was not just checking the address. She was not even just checking that my daughter's other mother wanted the letter. She knew there was a book. The only way Katrina could know there was a book was by opening the sealed envelope.

Katrina had opened my private mail. She had done so without first telling me this was what she was going to do. She opened my letter and read it, read my private letter about the grief I was experiencing.

I felt suddenly sick to my stomach. Not angry. I wanted to be angry but I felt too sick. And the sick feeling was what powerlessness feels like; it was a feeling, I realised, I knew quite well.

I rang Helen—being part-time, Katrina was not available that day—and Helen confirmed that it was possible the social worker had opened my letter and read it. Helen didn't know for sure, and she'd have the social worker ring me the next week. Helen said she was so sorry all this had gone so wrong for me; said she thought it was partly her fault, for some inane reason. She said she knew sorry wasn't enough. She should be a social worker, I thought. She was kind, could hear in my voice the degree of despair. She didn't talk like a custodian.

Katrina rang a week later and left a message. Helen told her I had concerns about the process, she said. Perhaps I could give her a call and we could talk. In the past, I would have called her back and had an angry interaction with her.

I would have left her in no doubt as to my view of her: she is incompetent, or worse; she really understands her use of the term custodian.

I didn't ring her back and yell. I didn't even return her call. Because what would it achieve? She opened the letter, she may have read it and I simply didn't want to know whether she was stupid or incompetent or mistaken or worked for a terrible organisation. I just wanted nothing to do with them.

When my daughter's other mother replied to me at my own address, she gave me her name and her address so I never had to write through the agency again.

I let go

SEVERAL WEEKS AFTER I SPOKE to Katrina, the records made by various people during my time in Melbourne arrived.

The records came in an unmarked envelope, along with a cheque for forty-five dollars because I had paid too much for them.

There was no explanation of the records, just a list of what was there. What explanation could anyone give? I thought later. There was no explanation.

⌒

The records from St Joseph's, possibly taken down by Jenny Fish, say I don't want the baby to go to English or Italian migrants. I don't remember saying this, but I don't disbelieve

I said it. My teacher's husband didn't like Italian and English people. I didn't want the baby to go to academic types either, the records say. Again, I don't remember saying this but I'm sure I said it. My teacher's husband hadn't started studying yet. He hated anyone who went to university. He said they didn't know anything about the real world, the world he knew about.

It made me realise what power my teacher and her husband had wielded in my life. I had taken on their views and made them my own. I have strong opinions and convictions and here I was, spouting the bigotry and anti-intellectualism of someone else. It shocked me to know that I was once so easily swayed. I am not so easily swayed these days.

In my records there should also be a description of the father, a bright young law student I loved but wasn't ready to marry. I don't know what happened to these records because I did tell Jenny Fish about this fictional father. I told many people about him. My teacher and her husband and I agreed I should. Maybe Jenny Fish didn't believe me so didn't write it down.

ᐸᐸ

The records from the hospital are hard to read, as if the writing itself was in a rush to be born. A babe female born at 4.40 pm, someone wrote. The doctor who'd said I'd have a long night of pain had been wrong.

The records say the cord was wrapped tightly around babe's neck; the word might be *twice* not *tightly*. I never knew this, twice or tightly.

Baby Ruth, they call her from then on. The records from the nursery at the hospital say that baby Ruth is posseting after feeds, has problems with wind, is crying in pain. The midwives change her formula, thicken it with cornflour, thin it, change it back, add gripe water at the end, treat constipation. Baby Ruth is still unsettled. She is admitted to St Joseph's Babies' Home thirteen days after I fly home to Brisbane.

When I read this, that baby Ruth spent thirteen days in a hospital nursery—waiting for a doctor's report that she was fit for adoption, I was struck by the fact that I didn't know—after she was born, after I left the hospital, when I got on the plane to fly home to Brisbane—where she was. She was my baby and I didn't know where she was. And I didn't ever ask.

Since I've given birth to Otis, I know what it is to be a mother. I know how every cell of your body is focused on this other life no matter what else tries to intervene. I know that in order not to know where Otis was in the minutes and hours and weeks following his birth I would have been physically restrained. He was where I was.

It had a profound effect on me, reading those records, because I understood, for the first time, how completely I shut out the reality of what happened.

Baby Ruth was unsettled, of course she was, because the one person she had a right, a birthright, to rely on was on a plane in a new size-twelve dress, heading to Brisbane, to her teacher and her teacher's husband.

⌒

At some time, baby Ruth went from St Joseph's Babies' Home to a foster home with a foster mother who said baby Ruth didn't smile. She was alert and serious and unhappy. She stayed in the foster home for thirty days, to give me time to change my mind.

I do remember being told about this. I remember I asked that it not happen, that baby Ruth go straight to her adoptive parents. I wanted there to be no delay. I didn't want a chance to change my mind. I didn't want baby Ruth to spend one more minute in the limbo of being baby Ruth than she had to. I wanted her new mother, her real mother, to drive to the hospital the day she was born and take her home.

There is a condition in which you can be pregnant and not know you are pregnant. I understand this condition. I had no concept of a human being inside me. I never ever ever thought of fingers or eyebrows. If there wasn't a baby, I wasn't leaving anything.

I was of course, and while my mind could think its thoughts, my body, my womb kept its dark secret. I had no idea of the grief that would come. But come it did, all these years later, to floor me. To punch me so hard in the jaw, in the solar plexus, as to leave me unable to breathe. Only my right leg keeps me upright, tilting this way and that in its corkscrew fashion.

Because, you see, when you give someone up like this, you must give everything up. You must not keep one small bit, not a hair, or a photograph, or a memory. If you do, it will eat you out, body and soul.

However much I tried to excuse myself, I was left with these bald facts, the facts I have had to accommodate:

It was my decision.

I was an adult in law.

I let go.

I did harm.

The way to live, I've discovered, is to let tears run through me like the sea, to swim in them, to surrender. I won't tell you I'm not responsible. I won't tell you I didn't know quite what I was doing or realise the consequences. I won't tell you because I want to tell the truth. I gave my child to strangers without a second thought.

⸺

After I read the records, I asked David to read them. He did and told me he felt raw. I felt raw too and it took some minutes before we understood our raw feelings were different. I felt raw because I had this baby, the baby, my baby, and what I did as a dead weight in my body.

But David saw this other baby—me, he said, too young to know my own mind, making a decision that even an old woman shouldn't have to make and then having to live with it. His sadness was like a beacon, a little light at the end of a darkness.

Byron cows

ON THE WEEKEND OF MY daughter's birthday last year, we came here to the farm. There had been so many birthdays when I'd felt nothing, but suddenly I was feeling everything.

With me, I brought half a brick, part of a ritual I was going through to unburden myself of a symbolic load I'd been carrying. All that grief was weighing me down, Stace said. I should find something heavy, put it in a bag and carry it around, let it go when I felt ready. It made sense at the time.

The week before, I'd filled a knapsack with two-and-a-half bricks from our backyard. I'd walked with the bricks up the hill to Birdwood Terrace. They seemed to get heavier with each step. I found myself in Toowong cemetery, where

I left the bricks under a tree. But I hadn't felt relieved. I'd felt bereft.

Not to anthropomorphise beyond what's reasonable for bricks, I'd gone back the next day and retrieved the half-brick and that's the one I took to the bay. The other two are in the cemetery still, as far as I know.

I walked along the beach with the half-brick in a calico bag, around my neck at first, and then against my chest, in my arms. I cried as I walked. It feels like a long time since I cared when people see me cry. I used to be quite self-conscious about it.

I walked from Main Beach to The Pass, meaning to swim with the half-brick and let it go some time in my swim, although I wasn't sure when. In the event, I swam out but the sea was rougher than it had first looked. I found myself being pushed towards the rocks on the seaward side of The Pass.

I heard my mother's voice calling out to the child me. 'Stick to the shallows or you'll be dashed against the rocks!' I felt I had to let go of the half-brick or myself, so I let go of the half-brick.

⌒

Yesterday afternoon as the light faded on the hill across from our cabin, I watched the cows that gathered on the grass. Otis bent down to the grass and chewed the way they chewed to show me what they were doing. Both of us could hear the munch of grass in their teeth. They seemed so contented.

Later, I heard them crying, those cows. They cried all night, deep throaty bellows nothing like the satisfied lowing I'd believed should come from creatures that had consumed so much grass. Their cries were more than sad; they were desperate. I thought perhaps it was the full moon.

When I asked the farm manager this morning, he told me the cows were crying for the calves that had been taken away from them. They were on their way to market to be veals.

I told Otis a bold-faced lie about why the cows cried. I said their calves would come back soon. Tonight I put my headphones on and listened to music. I couldn't bear to hear the noise.

You have had another birthday since we were last here. I wrote you a letter in which I said, If we don't meet again in our lifetimes, I have said what I needed to say.

In the first draft I wrote, If we don't meet in our lifetimes, *but I added 'again' because of course we did meet. You were in my body. My body gave birth to you.*

I often think of that sentence: If we don't meet again, I have said what I needed to say. *It has a way of calming me.*

The decision I made

IT WAS EARLY SPRING AT Thomas Street when I started
hearing voices in the night, or one voice, a child's voice,
crying, softly enough to be wind through a window crack on
the front veranda. It was not Otis; he was at the other end
of the house and the voice was older, sadder. Seven, I would
have said if forced to testify. The child was seven and alone
in suffering. If I sat up or got out of bed and concentrated
on them, the cries receded to nothing. I had to focus on
something else and they returned in the back of my mind.

David reminded me that it had been a bad year. I was
overwrought. But he didn't argue when I suggested we move
from the front bedroom. I told him I couldn't stand to sleep
near the veranda. He didn't even ask why.

You must understand I am not a believer, not even an agnostic. I would call spirits nonsense to their faces, would walk out of a séance, ignore a psychic. But there was something in the house, I felt sure now.

The people who lived at Thomas Street before us were a Catholic family, five children, a mother, father and two uncles who slept on the veranda. Devout, the neighbours on the near side said. I asked the woman who lived over the back, who'd lived there her whole life, if it was possible that ours had been an unhappy house. Yes, she said, it had. She would not say more despite my prompting and offering of tea, just changed the subject whenever I raised it.

⌒

I told Louise the whole story of what had happened in my young life, the guilt I was now feeling. I told Louise because she had been with me since the start and I needed her help. Before I told her, I worried she would judge me harshly. Once again, she did not. 'How could they?' she said. 'How could they do that to you?'

I told her sometimes I thought my life wasn't worth going on with. She sent me flowers and a card. *You're going to pull through this*, she wrote. *You will, and David and Otis and I will make sure you do.*

Louise started visiting more often, sitting with me, with Otis. She never once suggested I shouldn't be the mother of a child, even though it was something I was becoming certain of. I was frightened that if people knew what was happening in our house, if they knew how I would fall apart and not manage, they would come and take Otis away from me. It was for a time my biggest fear, that I would lose Otis too.

I told Louise, 'You kept your child, I gave mine to strangers.'

Like me, Louise had fallen pregnant unintentionally as a young woman. Her circumstances were completely different, as she reminded me. She and her baby's father, Gerard, were going to marry sometime anyway. It just sped things up. But it was still the truth. She held on to her baby. I gave mine to strangers.

My friend Louise stayed with me through all of the years I was of no use to the world. At times we lost contact—my fault, not hers—and our values don't always mesh on things. She invested everything in four children and a house needing renovation and cars and life in private schools. I invested in a career of sorts and at any rate could not cope with too much time around her children, around her babies. When their son Josh had his twenty-first, I couldn't bear to go. I wrote him a letter I never sent.

Dear Josh,

I was sorry to be away for your coming of age. It's a milestone for you I'd have loved to share in. Were you the barista? If so, I am doubly sorry to have missed the occasion.

When I was eighteen, I became pregnant. I gave the baby, a girl I named Ruth, up for adoption. She has lived a happy enough life as far as I know. I believed I was doing the only thing I could.

When Louise told me she was pregnant with you, she was not much older than I was when I was pregnant, not much older than you are now. Your mother has such courage, Josh, and such conviction. Nothing would take you away from her. She is one of the best people I know.

Your life has been a blessing for me in ways you can't have understood. Once, when you were about two, I was sitting on the floor and you came and sat by me and put your hand on my leg like we were buddies. You just sat there. For you it was just what you did, but for me it was an acknowledgement of me as a person in your little life.

I have no advice to give you Josh, just a hope that the rest of this life will be rich and full.

He is a fine boy, Josh. They are a fine family.

⌒

For a time, I feared the presence in our house for presentiment, a future rather than past evil; evil would be done to a child of seven here, and that child was Otis. We should move away, I told David, move anywhere to make sure Otis remains safe. Even as I said it, I knew this for what it was, my poor worn-out imagination, just as I knew I would not die on the Golden Gate Bridge or be taken by a shark while swimming in the bay yet still feared them.

In my kahuna sessions with Stace, we started to feel the presence of Mary, the mother of Jesus, with us. This did not seem odd.

I asked Mary, a mother who lost a child, to intercede on my behalf, to talk to God about giving me my life back, so I could mother my son. 'You already have your life,' she said, smiling. 'Look, don't you see?'

For a while, I saw my fear of bridges as a metaphor. Terrified, I walked from pylon to pylon, experienced a measure of safety, and then set out again. But at times, it felt as if there would be no end to this, no Sausalito. It was like labour; labour that could not end in birth. After Otis was born, I wanted another child. I longed for another child. But the child I longed for was baby Ruth, who was gone. She could not be born, that is the truth. She could not be reborn. I could not atone. And so I laboured.

I was put on Earth to make one decision. I made the wrong decision. For a long time, I could not get past this.

⌒

Mary was a friend of a friend who came to the hospital after Otis was born. She had five adult children and had trained as a social worker after her kids grew up. She'd worked with teenage parents. Mary took an interest in new mothers, in me and little Otis. I put the yellow stuffed toy dragon she gave Otis in his cot with him after we got home from the hospital, along with Blue Bear, given to him by Louise. The brand of the dragon is Gund, German, and that became the dragon's name. To me, it meant that good mothers were watching over him. The nightjars notwithstanding, surely Gund and Blue Bear, from mothers like Mary and Louise, would keep him safe.

I gave Mary a copy of the essay I'd written about birth. It was the first time I'd put in writing that I'd had a baby before Otis, and before it was published I sent it to everyone in my life who hadn't known. I sat down with many of my friends, including Kim, and told them in person. I didn't tell them everything, not then, but it was the beginning of telling the secret. It was terrifying, as every step on this journey has been, and it turned out all right, as every step on this journey has.

Before the essay was published, I emailed Mary and told her I'd had a baby as a teenager and I wanted to let her know before the essay came out because she'd been so kind to me when Otis was born and I'd felt dishonest not telling her the truth.

Some months later, Mary called me and we met for coffee. She told me she already knew I'd had a baby earlier in my life. I asked her how.

Her daughter in Melbourne, she said carefully, was going out with a boy, and the boy was my daughter's cousin. My daughter had told the boy that her biological mother was from Brisbane, and she told him my name. Mary's daughter knew my name because Mary had mentioned me.

Her daughter and this boy were about to marry, Mary said.

This was such a strange coincidence I could only believe it must have come from something beyond us.

We met again. I told Mary there would be no rules from my side about what she said or didn't say. There would be no rules from me. I don't believe in secrets.

⌐

Mary and I became closer. She was someone I could lean on in those months I felt so treacherous. In all the time she worked with young parents, she said, she only ever met one family where the baby might have been better off somewhere else. It felt like truth to me at a time when everyone else in my life was serving up platitudes—you did the best thing, she was better off, you made the right decision.

'And even then,' Mary said, 'you'd have to be sure before you took a baby from his mother.'

It was a relief to hear someone say it.

I said, 'Mary, I was put on Earth to make one decision. I made the wrong decision.' I was crying, had been crying for months. Whenever I told people this, they said, 'Of course you didn't. You did the best thing for your baby,' which I knew to be untrue.

Mary looked me in the eye directly, which was rare for Mary. She mostly let you slide away. 'You made a wrong decision,' she said. 'You probably did. That's okay. You've made others. You'll make more.'

What happens to women

I COULD WRITE AN ESSAY on adoption, the harm the policy we had here in Australia did to those women who gave their babies to strangers, to those babies who found themselves in a different place from their kin, to adopting parents who believed they were given a blank slate to write on. We were cheated, all of us, when we were told taking a baby from a mother had no effect.

Australia is one of the few countries that decided in the 1960s to make adoption secret. In other places, parents could have an ongoing relationship with their children. In Australia this was not an option, because social policy makers felt it was important there be a clean break. Mothers were not encouraged to spend time with their newborn children. Everything was secret. When state legislatures were moving to change their adoption acts so that children and parents could have access to information and each other, some people objected very strongly.

But I am in the frame when it comes to adoption so I am probably not a person to write in this area. Having said that, I have no hard and fast views about adoption itself. Would I want a child to spend a life in foster care, or be adopted into a family where they might thrive? Would I want a child to grow up in an institution, or with parents who love them?

My complaint would not be with adoption. My complaint would be against any system that offers no alternative to women who find themselves pregnant.

The system we had in place for adoption when I gave my baby to strangers is the same kind of system every woman comes up against today when she has a baby, the system of maternity care. Our choices are limited. This is an area I feel very comfortable writing about, the ways we control what happens to women's bodies.

⌐⌐

I worked on a review of maternity services in Queensland in 2005. I read the submissions from women, some of whom had had the most horrendous experiences of birth as a result of their care. Women whose babies died were cared for in the same ward as women whose babies lived. They'd hear babies cry all night, watch new mothers breastfeed them. They'd have to explain over and over again to the staff who asked them when they were due or how their baby was that yes, they'd already had a baby, but their baby had died. When I asked the midwives in the hospital why these women couldn't be cared for in another place, they said, 'They've had a baby. They have to be in a ward where there are midwives, not nurses.'

'Couldn't the midwives go to them?'

'I suppose so, but that's not very practical.'

Women were bullied by obstetricians because they did or didn't want a particular kind of pain relief during labour. One woman had an episiotomy the midwife described as a 'hindquarter resection' because the obstetrician was in a bad mood with the woman; she had a birth plan. As a matter of routine, women had their babies taken from them and placed in nurseries where they were fed formula when the women wanted more than anything to breastfeed. Or women were treated as pariahs by midwives because they had decided not to breastfeed. Women were punished and abused and neglected because they wanted something, anything; to hold their babies straight after birth, to bury their placenta under a full moon, to save their cord blood, to cry.

I did not connect what happened to these women in 2005 with what happened to me in the 1980s. But it is drawn from the same wellspring, that cruelty to the most vulnerable in order to impose your own belief system—by force if necessary, by hindquarter resection.

Centacare, the Catholic agency through which I gave my child away to strangers, still advertises adoption services for women. I can't imagine a girl like me going down that path today, but if she did I would tell her to go back, spend some time with her baby, reconsider. If she then decided she wanted to relinquish her parenting rights, then of course she should be able to. But according to my friend Mary, very few do when given a chance to weigh up both options. At any rate, I would be unable to tell her what the pros of giving her baby to strangers are. Someone else would have to do that. I no longer know what the pros of giving a baby to strangers are.

The energy that led to church and state adoptions, that led to a position where it was always better to give a baby to a married childless couple than let a single mother raise a child, is the I–thou attitude of righteous people every-where. It is as healthy now as it was when I gave baby Ruth to strangers. It is particularly rampant when it meets up with women's health and vulnerability around the birth of children, or when it finds itself responsible for any kind of care of vulnerable people. There are midwives and doctors and carers out there who still know best what women and children want and need.

I have a friend who has just had her first baby. She is in the throes of wonder about this miracle that has come into her life. She is vulnerable, soft and needs encouragement, as we all do at that time. My friend visited a health clinic and was told by the child health nurse that her breastfed baby had failed to regain birth weight. 'What are you doing with her?' the nurse said. My friend tried to tell her and was interrupted mid-sentence. 'Goodness me. Wake her every two hours and make her feed. Come back Friday and if she hasn't improved, we'll start some formula.' She destroyed my friend's confidence as a mother for a little while and she was wrong, wrong in heart and wrong in fact.

At some stage during my work with Stace, I had a rebirthing session with a woman from Ocean Shores. It does not seem strange to be saying this, as if I have rebirthing sessions with women from Ocean Shores every other week; I do not, incidentally. She helped me immensely, the woman from Ocean Shores, partly because of how resistant I was to her and her beliefs, her assumptions.

I spent two hours regressed on a couch. Beforehand I wondered how I'd fill the time, but it ended in seconds, before I had finished. My body shook. My teeth chattered. This is fear, I would have said to the woman if I could have got the words out, fear like you've never known.

Afterwards, she said she was sure there was anaesthetic at my birth, or at baby Ruth's birth, or even Otis's. I was never sure who we were rebirthing. There was anaesthetic because she became drowsy. The anaesthetic was leaking out of me, she said.

Her own birth was traumatic, she said, because she believed she had murdered her mother.

'Did your mother die?' I said.

'No,' she said. 'But I thought she did.'

'Wow,' I said, not knowing what else to say.

Over time, I have begun to place what happened to me in its context. But what I took away from my rebirthing session with the woman from Ocean Shores was nothing to do with birth, and nothing to do with baby Ruth, which surprised me. I took that picture of myself at ten, standing beside the pool. It came back to me that day at Ocean Shores and it has been with me since. I am fierce with life in that picture; that's the point. I am here, she is saying. I am here.

I'd rather be happy than normal

ONE NIGHT, NOT LONG AFTER I told Louise the truth about my teacher and her husband, I was organising Otis for his bath and found sand all through his bed. It had leaked from the rolled-up cuffs of his pants when he was playing on the bed earlier. It had probably been collected at kindy that day and I hadn't noticed.

It shouldn't have been a big deal but what happened on that beach at Redcliffe had come back as a memory around this time. It was a memory that came back whole, formed, while my body shook with the fear of it. I couldn't talk to anyone about it yet, but everything felt too much, even the noise of a normal child, the light of a normal day.

Feelings which would overwhelm me had been pressing down all day. When I discovered that poor little Otis had spilled sand in his bed accidentally, I was furious. I told him I was sick and tired of the mess he made. I said other things I'm not going to write here.

Otis retaliated, started spreading sand on the bathroom floor. I picked him up and carried him back into his room and put him on his sandy bed to have some time out. I was still yelling. He was crying.

It was me who needed the time out. When I'd calmed enough, I went back to him and said I was sorry. I said that when he put sand on the bathroom floor, maybe it was his way of saying my anger hadn't been fair.

He nodded hard through sobs.

I told him he was right to do what he did, that when someone didn't treat him fairly, he must speak up, must have it named. I told him that I was not really angry anyway, I was sad, that it was nothing to do with him, that I was sorry. I said I would not always be like this.

After he went to bed I got in the shower and let the tears come.

⌣

An afternoon not long after this, we were in the backyard, trying to talk our poor trees into growing. There were three of them. We'd picked them out at the nursery when we'd bought our house with its yard. Otis had a jacaranda, mine

227

was a coolamon, and David's was a dwarf macadamia. We'd planted flowers too, although they hadn't bloomed, and herbs, but the rats had made short work of them.

Otis was wearing his favourite pants, brown cords gone in both knees, with his starry night pyjamas under, his pink gumboots. He was digging a hole where the chook pens had been. I was always slightly worried he'd dig up more asbestos.

Late in the afternoon, I sat down with him on the grass and said I wanted to tell him something important. I wanted to explain why I'd been sad and sometimes angry. He looked at me with his serious face, big eyes focused on mine.

'I had a baby girl when I was very young,' I said.

He didn't say anything.

'It was a long time ago,' I said, 'a long time before you were born.'

He nodded slowly.

'I was too young then to look after a baby,' I said. 'Otherwise, I would have looked after her because I love being a mummy.'

He didn't smile, continued to regard me solemnly.

'The baby grew up with another mummy and daddy. They very much wanted children and couldn't have their own,' I said. 'That sometimes happens.'

I did not cry as I spoke.

'Of course, this would never happen to you,' I said, 'because I am much older now, old enough to look after you.'

Sometimes, I explained, there was sadness in my body where the baby was, and the sadness needed to come out. That's all. But I wasn't as good at feeling my feelings as he was, so I didn't always know how to let it out. He'd taught me a lot about that, I said.

When I didn't let them out, the feelings would build up like a pot boiling on my head and sometimes the lid blew off the pot.

'I yell at you, like I did last night,' I said.

He nodded in recognition.

'But it's not anything to do with you. It's to do with me. And I'm sorry. What I really need is to go away for a little while and cry and then I feel better. And that's what I've been trying to do now when I feel sad.'

We sat for a while looking at our sad garden. I said if he had any questions, he could ask them any time he wanted.

He looked at me. 'When you cry, can you leave the door open?'

'I shut the door because I don't want to upset you,' I said.

'What would upset me?' he said. 'You're the one who's upset.'

'Of course,' I said. I wondered how someone so young could teach so much.

'The girl is now a grownup,' I said.

I told him your name.

'She's your sister,' I said.

'I know that,' he said, and went back to his digging.

⌒

The morning of that same day, before I'd told him about his sister, Otis and I had had another conversation, about a sandal he'd lost that he was really upset about. To put his feelings in context, I'd told him a story about a puppy I'd had once that had run away. I said I'd felt the same kind of sadness he was feeling about his sandal so I understood.

The next day, getting ready for kindy, he said, 'You know that baby, Mummy?'

'Yes?'

'Was it a puppy?'

Humour may not translate in such difficult circumstances, but to me, his simple understanding of the world is like taking a breath. I wish I could put it in a bottle and drink it every morning.

⌒

After I wrote to my daughter's other mother and sent her the essay I wrote on birth, she wrote back. She'd found birth hard to relate to, she said. It was something she'd never experienced and when women shared their stories, she didn't feel she could really understand.

When I read her letter, I realised how insensitive it was to send her an essay on birth. It hadn't even occurred to me that she too had experienced loss; she had wanted to have children and had never given birth.

I replied, *You and I are on different corners of this fraught human triangle and it is too easy for me to focus on my own corner, to shore it up and make it sharp.*

In her next letter, she changed the shape. *I see myself somewhere along a straight line between you and Miranda. Sooner or later (sooner I hope) my job will be to get out of the way so that you two can grow closer.*

A few weeks after I told him about his sister, Otis said, 'You know, Mummy, I think it was good you gave away that other baby.'

'Why's that?'

'Well, because her other mummy and daddy, they couldn't have a baby and then they had one.'

⌒

We worked for two years at Thomas Street with our architect and builder. We developed over a dozen renovation plans and then a new house design for the site. Nothing worked. Nothing. And nothing ever grew there, not our trees, not even our son.

We sold the house, finally, to a couple who did up old houses and made them look like old houses but work like new ones. I dug up our three trees and we put them in pots and took them with us.

Before the new owners signed the contract, I said to the real estate agent: 'Tell them that there is a presence in that house. I want you to make sure they know.' I am no longer willing to keep secrets.

Target

I RESEARCHED SEXUAL MISCONDUCT WHEN I was writing my novel *No Safe Place*, which is about a young woman at university who says a student counsellor sexualised their counselling relationship. I went to a conference at the University of Sydney where I heard the accounts of women and men who had been sexually abused by teachers and priests and therapists who put their own sexual needs before their duty of care.

The harm was terrible. I saw how those people at the conference, some who'd been abused as children, others as teenagers or adults, shook with emotion. Most had not been able to fulfil their potential, their years marked by addiction, self-harm, an inability to form lasting relationships. Some were gone already. They'd taken their own lives, and a family member was telling their story. It was shocking to me what these people had suffered. It frightened me, if I'm honest.

I can remember thinking at the time that what happened to them was not the same as what happened in my life. I am not a victim of anything, I told myself. I will not call myself a victim. I will not call my teacher and her husband perpetrators. Words like that made me uncomfortable. Surely if there was fault here it belonged with me. I brought it upon myself. I'd been a troubled teen. They had helped me. Wasn't that what happened?

Later, I wanted desperately to believe I had agency, choice. My first therapist, Mick, was at pains to make me see the world this way. I gave them a special power to hurt me. I could take my power back. I spent a long time thinking this way.

⌣

Wayne, the therapist I went to see after I accidentally hurt Otis with the stroller clip, became exasperated only once in the time we were meeting. I'd maintained my view that what had happened with my teacher and her husband was my responsibility, that I'd been the one who'd done wrong, or I'd given them my power, as Mick said, and I could take it back. Wayne and I had come up against this more than once.

'I'm sorry,' he said this particular day. 'But I just don't see that you gave them a special power to hurt you.' He was quoting me quoting Mick. 'I don't see that you had any power at all. I really don't.' He was shaking his head in frustration.

Wayne had asked me, when I'd first gone to see him and told him about the counselling I'd already done, why I hadn't gone back to see Mick. I told him that David and I had become friends with Mick and Mick's wife Suzi. We had even gone to their wedding.

Mick became friends with many of his clients. When I started reading about sexual misconduct to research *No Safe Place*, I learned that counsellors are not supposed to make friends with their clients. It's one of those relationships where power is unequal. At the time, it didn't bother me, as Mick had never misused our relationship for his own gain.

Although Wayne never said anything about this, over time, I began to realise that Mick's way of seeing the world suited him, but he was wrong about me. He was wrong to believe that, at sixteen, I gave my teacher and her husband, a couple in their late twenties with much more life experience than me, my power. He was wrong that my teacher, who had a duty of care, was just like any other person in my life. And he was wrong to befriend me.

When Suzi left Mick some years ago, she and I remained friends. I knew she and Mick had got together when she was twenty-one and he was forty. But he was also her work supervisor when they met, she told me. And, I learned, he had been counselling her on a personal level. He had mixed a work relationship, a counselling relationship and a sexual relationship with someone who had much less life experience.

Suzi has been one of the few people in my life who understands, at a visceral level, some of what happened to me. It happened to her too.

⁓

There's not much nuance in the language we have to describe sexual misconduct and there's probably not a lot of nuance in the reality either. There are victims and perpetrators and rape is always rape, as Stace once said to me. But while courts try to apportion blame based on age and maturity, coercion and consent, people like me who've actually experienced this kind of betrayal can no longer live the trusting lives we might have. I think this has been the hardest thing, learning to trust again that people won't betray me.

Still, I remained uncomfortable describing my relationship with my teacher and her husband as sexual abuse, and I was uncomfortable describing what happened to me on the beach at Redcliffe as rape. I was sixteen when the relationship started, the age of consent in Queensland. I'd consented to everything that happened, hadn't I? And the memory of the beach came much later than the event itself, however clearly it came. And anyway, I had sex with my teacher's husband after I came home from Melbourne. So does the rape count? As for my teacher, I loved my teacher, and I thought she loved me.

The American novelist and essayist Mary Gaitskill wrote an essay in *HQ* about two experiences. In the first, she was overwhelmed by a man in the street who dragged her into a dark alley and raped her. In the second, she was on a date and said no to sex. The man raped her. When she told her friend, she said this second experience of rape felt worse than the first, that she wasn't even sure she could call it rape. Her friend said, 'You were raped, all right—you raped yourself.' Mary Gaitskill said she didn't like hearing her friend say this, but she also knew that it was true. *I raped myself. I raped myself.* There's something in this that felt true to me, not in terms of rape but in terms of the entire relationship with my teacher and her husband. How did I let myself, a strong young woman on her way to the world, get waylaid by these people who were bound to cause me harm? How did I not see? How did I not protect myself? Why did I go along with what they were doing for so long?

It must be very difficult for courts to apportion blame in cases where young adults or adults have been in these relationships. I cannot now understand what I saw in my teacher and her husband. In those years of my late teens, it was something akin to a cult, where the people I saw and the actual people were a long way apart, but I didn't know that, and I was so isolated that no one else was providing an alternative view. My teacher was my teacher and then a leader of religious curriculum development. Her husband was an officer in the army. Their status in the community legitimised them, legitimised what they did, so that even in my mind, it became me, the troubled teenager, who did wrong, not them. I believed this for years. And my family; we were not a 'normal' family, as I've said. I think shame fit me snugly. It wasn't until I met someone like David, until Brian met my teacher's husband, until I saw Wayne in therapy, that I started to see an alternative view.

When I have told my story—and I have had to tell it to many people now, people who have known me for years and known none of it—some people say they believe me innocent and my teacher and her husband guilty. They shake their heads and say they can't believe those people could have done what they did. I'm not sure if they say it to be kind, or if they really do think my teacher and her husband are evil people. But I can't join with my friends, even knowing everything I know now.

I have said this is my story. I am the point-of-view character, the unreliable narrator of my own life. I think if this story were told from another point of view, those friends who vilify my teacher and her husband might see things differently. For instance, as I read back over what I have written, I see I have made much of the fact that we agreed we would not tell anyone I was pregnant to protect my teacher's husband's commission. This is true from my point of view, and it looks cowardly of my teacher's husband. But for him, I am sure it was galling to lie. He was generally a loyal and courageous person who owned his mistakes. He already had a wife. She was unwell, potentially unable to bear children, and vulnerable. He stuck by his wife, the first promise he'd made, and left me, to whom he'd made no promise, to cope alone.

This may just be the novelist in me who can always see at least two sides of a situation, or the last remnants of the cult-like brainwashing I suffered, but if we could go down to the beach at Redcliffe that night from my teacher's husband's point of view, I know we would see an entirely different scene. I suspect he wouldn't even recognise himself the way I have written him. He would think I was writing about another experience, another him, another me. She was there, he would say, a willing partner in consummating our relationship. She had a great time. In his story, we both lost control because we were really living. My teacher's husband used to say that some people remain on the sidelines their whole lives, never take risks, watch, criticise. 'If you really live,' he said, 'and I mean *really* live, you make mistakes, but you also do some good.' I think he believed this.

⸺

So what were these two relationships then, from their point of view? A teacher unsure of her own sexuality becoming involved with a young student? A woman whose husband's needs are overwhelming? A woman wanting to help a student and things go wrong? And my teacher's husband. A rapist? A man losing control? A well-meaning but deeply damaged man doing damage to someone else?

I read a paper put out by the US Congress, gathering the research that's been done into educator sexual misconduct. That's what they call it when teachers have sex with students. They spent a good deal of time on the terminology, considered 'sexual abuse' rather than 'misconduct', but decided this put too much emphasis on the victim and whether they suffered harm, rather than on the teacher and his or her conduct. The matter of what to name students was considered too. 'Targets', they decided. 'Complainant' made it sound legal and alleged, 'victim' took away a student's power. Target, because they were targeted.

In a way, it doesn't much matter what terminology I use, or what the motivations of my teacher or her husband were. They did harm, great harm, and to more than one person. There are children born from the relationships here, children who don't have a choice where they've come from, children who one way or another have to live with the consequences of other people's actions. My daughter, my son. Their daughter.

At the conference in Sydney, I listened to Dr Carolyn Quadrio, a psychiatrist who still works with victims of sexual abuse. Dr Quadrio spoke angrily of the harm that had been done, the perpetrators who offended again and again, the lack of safeguards, the sense of betrayal. 'If you could under-stand what such a betrayal of trust means to someone, you would make sure it never happened again,' she said. Her drive and energy made the world feel safer.

In much of the research I did in order to write *No Safe Place* and to understand what happened to me, I found the disturbing fact that adults who have sex with children and young people offend more than once. When I read this, I thought back on my teacher, her husband, wondered if there were other young people like me they harmed, people who didn't know what they didn't know. I wished I'd understood the harm earlier, realised how young I was. It might have meant I made a complaint to someone, perhaps even helped someone else.

※

Last year, I read a self-help book that suggested I sit around a campfire in my mind with my teacher and her husband and try to understand them. I did this, mentally sat around that imaginary campfire with my imaginary teacher and her husband. In my head, my teacher's husband told me he'd been sexually abused as a boy by a family friend. My imaginary teacher told me she'd been abused by her alcoholic father. They were just plain damaged, same as all of us. They were not bad people. They were deeply flawed. They didn't set out to make me responsible for what we did. They just didn't have the courage to live, despite what they thought about themselves.

My teacher and her husband asked me to keep secrets that have done harm. They took my voice as a young woman, took it for all these years. They contributed fundamentally to a situation where I was faced, as a young woman, with a decision, a Sophie's choice, to give my child to strangers.

I spent my twenties and thirties living a short distance from my body, like Joyce's Mr Duffy. I was in my forties and the mother of another child before I began to close that distance.

~

I have to let my teacher and her husband go, or be consumed by them. I have to let them go, dive in with that ten-year-old girl, put one arm up and over, the other arm up and over, and breathe. In this way, I go forward in the water, I swim.

Unresolved grief

THERE WAS A STORY IN the newspaper a while back about a mother who was out jogging with her baby in a stroller. She stopped along a riverside track because her phone rang.

When the woman finished her call and turned, the baby was gone. She searched the track, the roadway and then called the police. 'My baby has been taken!' she screamed into the phone. The police found the child, the stroller, in the river twenty minutes later. The child was dead.

My friends were critical of the woman. 'She didn't put on the brake, you know,' one said, with anger in her eyes. 'How could you walk away from a stroller?' another said. Still another friend said: 'Oh, please. The first thing you'd do would be to check the stroller hadn't slipped; you wouldn't think someone had stolen your baby.' (The woman was well known. It was not out of the question that someone would take her baby.)

I am floored by their hatred, their damnation of the woman. I understand it too. We all wish we had a foot on that stroller brake, a hand on the strap, an arm around the child. We see him slip away into the river and think, No, no, this must not be. I understand these women want to save a child.

But I am not with them. I think of the mother with sadness, for whatever she says on national television afterwards, I know her life will not be the life it would have been. It will not resemble that other life in any way. She is already someone new. She has grown a different skin.

I look at the photograph of Otis and me on the beach, the one David took at Byron. On that weekend, for the first time since Otis was small, I started to believe I might be all right. We would walk along the beach in the evening and the sea and wind would take my tears and make them less important, part of the afternoon rather than something to be revered or feared. Otis would run and look for shells and jellyfish. David was taking photographs again.

I can look at that photo of Otis and me and place us in a context, understand that I might have been the woman who gave her baby to strangers, but that I was also this other woman who had a child she could love and care for.

I spent a long wasted time wishing this hadn't happened, wishing I'd been more self-preserving, self-respecting or whatever other girls were. I never quite knew how other girls managed their lives so well. I have never been able to manage my life well. I did wish I could have done something differently to stop what happened to me from happening.

My right leg used to give me messages. It took a long time for me to hear them. I listen to my body now, the pain behind my heart that tells me to let go, the ache in my jaw that tells me I am angry.

I have learned, too, to say sorry to Otis, to tell him I was wrong, unfair. I have had to say sorry a lot these past few years. I am getting quite good at it.

I would say to him as often as I'd think to, When I am sad, it is nothing to do with you. It is not your fault.

One day, when David found me crying, Otis came up behind him and said, 'Don't worry, Daddy, it's nothing to do with you. It is not your fault.'

⌒

David has put meaning to the phrases we never included in our marriage vows: 'in sickness and in health, in good times and in bad'. He has taken the weight of our family onto his slight shoulders and continued walking down the road, with me, with Otis. He has been with me over twenty years and says he doesn't look like going anywhere else. At times I have told him to leave. I have said to get out of the house. I have told him that he doesn't understand me, for he doesn't, and how could he? How could anyone who wasn't there? He stays with me and waits out the storm, tells me I'm right, he doesn't understand, but he'll do anything he can to help.

Sometimes still it is too much to have him near me. My teeth chatter. My body shudders with fear. I cannot abide another being beside me. But eventually, mostly, I can bear him nearby and then his hand on my back, him holding me in his arms. I take comfort in his touch. It is another kind of surrender, this finding my lover again.

⌒

I have nothing to offer women whose children are gone, not even that loss passes. This has not been my experience. It has not passed. I wrote in a letter to my daughter that while facing great pain has brought many more tears, it also brings the beauty of the world more sharply into focus. And while this might be true, some days it is not enough.

I have been on the internet to google women like me. They are crazy, most of them, crazy like me. They list the crimes against themselves, take governments and churches to court, write theses, invent terms like 'unresolved grief'. They cycle on the bikeway listening to 'The Long Road' and yell and cry along.

I have learned less than I would have liked given how long I have been here in the past with baby Ruth. I have learned this: at those times when I can look at my life without guilt or blame or anger, when I can even be kind, I have found a measure of my power. The hardest thing for me has been to face that at some level this was a choice, a choice I made. Perhaps it wasn't for others, who were coerced, threatened, frightened into complying. They are welcome to the high moral ground. I am not among them there.

⌐

After we moved out of Thomas Street, we rented a brick townhouse that looked towards the city. At that time, we were still planning to build a new house on the Thomas Street site. Once we moved into the rental and I saw how much happier it was, we put Thomas Street on the market. When it sold, I started looking for a new house.

I hadn't planned even to look at the house we eventually bought because it faced west at the back—hot in Brisbane—and was on the southern side of a hill, so wouldn't get the predominant north-easterly breezes. I was only in the street because I was looking at the house opposite. The house we bought was open at the time so I went to look.

I spent five minutes in the house, drove home so that David could look while it was still open, called the agent that night, met him at the house on Monday morning with Otis so Otis could give his vote and then made an offer.

The agent hadn't known David was my husband when David had gone through the house, so when I said that since my five-year-old son wanted to buy the house, I wanted the agent to take my offer to the owners, he asked me, casually, did my husband know I was offering on a house? I think he wondered about my sanity.

We love our little house. It is a house you can come home to.

Byron moon

LAST NIGHT WE SAW THE moon rising at the end of the main street of the little town of Bangalow, an enormous red ball coming out of the land like a hot-air balloon. We ate at a restaurant and Otis saw a candle burning for a boy who'd worked in the restaurant; the boy had been killed on his motorcycle and the candle would burn for forty days, as is the Greek tradition. Otis wanted to know how you could die on a motorcycle and I did my best to tell him.

You don't realise until you are a parent that you will have to lie. I have promised I will tell the truth. I have tried to be honest with Otis. I am afraid of dishonesty. I know it can harm much more than it helps. I know now what secrets do to people, how they cauterise from within. But I lie to Otis.

I mediate the world because I know it may be too much for him.

A dog followed us almost all the way home through the dark streets of the town. It was broad-chested and stocky and it had no road sense but wouldn't let me lead it. I walked as close as I dared—I have a fear of dogs, having been bitten half a dozen times as a child—and hailed cars to slow down as they approached. It would have been run over three or four times had I not remained near.

David and Otis kept asking me why I was letting the dog come with us.

'What will we do with a dog?' David said.

'Is it really friendly?' from Otis.

I knew the cottage wasn't equipped for animals. I didn't exactly have a plan but felt sure one would present itself.

As we turned into the street where we'd parked, a car I was hailing to slow pulled up. It was the dog's owner, who had been searching frantically. The dog had escaped through an unlatched gate and had walked all the way to town. 'I have a little boy too,' she said after she'd snuggled the dog into its front seat bed. 'That's why he followed you. He thought your little boy was like my little boy and might know the way home. He'd have been killed if he hadn't followed you, sweetie,' she said to Otis.

Afterwards, Otis told the story of how we'd saved the dog's life. 'He thought I was his little boy,' Otis would tell people. 'That's why he stayed with us.'

⸎

This morning when I swam, I went out through The Pass and around the rocks. The water was a dense green so I couldn't see more than a few inches in front or below me. It made me afraid, this new blindness. The sea was calm, like a rocking crib, and still I was afraid. My fingers and ankles found bits of seaweed that startled me because I had no idea what they were.

I wanted to see, to know what was around me. I wanted to know.

⸎

Just before we came away on this trip, I was walking with my friend Cass. We walk once maybe twice a week up a hill near where I live. We call the hill a mountain because it makes us feel better. After we walk up our mountain, we have coffee.

After I hurt Otis with the stroller clip, Cass rang me every week, kept ringing if I didn't call back. She told me it was not normal to get in the shower every morning and cry. Her niece, a physician, said it was not normal. She knew a psychiatrist, she said, the eighty-six-year-old father of a friend. At eighty-six, he'd have seen it all, she said. Maybe he could help.

'Before you do anything drastic,' she said once, although I hadn't mentioned anything drastic, 'will you call me?' 'Yes,' I said. 'Good,' she said.

While walking on our mountain on the morning before we came away, I was telling Cass about my conversation with Mary, how much it had meant to me, how it had helped to have someone acknowledge that I'd made the wrong decision.

By this time, I was travelling much better. Cass and I would walk up our mountain and watch the sun and hear the mad cockatoos. We'd even spied an eagle's nest that year, the baby eagles well protected by their fierce mother.

Cass stopped on the track. 'I don't think I agree with that, Mary-Rose,' she said. 'No, I don't at all. How could anyone know that? How could anyone be sure? You don't know what your daughter's life would have been like. You can't have any idea.' She was shaking her head.

It occurred to me suddenly that Cass was right, just as Mary had been right. I made a wrong decision. Yes, I did. There is no way of knowing if I made a wrong decision. Yes again. Whatever baby Ruth's life had become, it wasn't the life she would have had with me. That was all I could really know for sure.

⌐

Not everyone in my life has agreed I should write this story. After I hurt Otis in the stroller clip, I had stopped writing anything at all and when I started again, I found myself writing the truth about what happened to me as a young woman.

During this time, I had been meeting with my friend Kris Olsson to workshop what we were each writing. We used to

meet after my cold-water swimming at South Bank for breakfast, but for a long time I hadn't had anything to workshop.

After I started writing again, I read out loud to Kris what
I'd written. We sat there in the winter sun crying together.

Some time later, Fiona Stager from Avid Reader Bookstore
in Brisbane hosted an event where I read from an essay I'd
written for *Griffith Review*, published by Julianne Schultz,
telling some of the secrets I'd kept. It was terrifying, and I
was glad I did it.

If these women hadn't been willing, I would never have
kept writing.

⟶

Some of my friends said I should not under any circumstances
share the story of what happened to me, to us, with my
daughter. It is too much for a child to bear, even in adulthood,
they said. Others said some secrets are better kept. Past is
past. Leave it there.

I do not agree with them. I agree with my friend Cass.

'Of course she has a right to know,' Cass said. 'We all
have the right to information. People make me sick the way
they hide things, as if information can harm a person.'

It's secrets that harm a person. I know this much now.

⟶

I had resumed contact with my daughter's other mother. I had
written a version of this story. I wanted to explain to my

daughter how I arrived on a dark beach on the night of her conception, and how I came to leave her with strangers.

I would rather have sat down and told her in person, but that was not an option. I knew it was entirely possible that it might never be an option—many children adopted at birth decide not to meet those who gave them away. My daughter had not expressed interest in any contact with me. I wanted to tell her the truth.

I sent the story through my daughter's other mother, which was still the only way to contact my daughter. I asked her other mother to pass the story on. I told her I wanted my daughter to have the information, that I didn't want anything from my daughter but I wanted her to have the information.

This is not your story, and perhaps there will be some comfort in that. It is not even half of the story of where you come from and it is none of the story of where you are going. You came through me on your own journey. This is mine. You can take what is useful from it and move on. I read Women Who Run with the Wolves: *'The wild woman carries with her the bundles for healing; she carries everything a woman needs to be and know. She carries the medicine for all things.'*

My daughter's other mother rang me, out of the blue. I heard her voice for the first time on my answering machine, this woman I'd been corresponding with on and off for over twenty years, this woman who is my daughter's mother. She'd read my story, she said, and she wanted to talk to me. She didn't leave a number, just a time she'd call again.

When she called again, she said she had decided to read the story before she told Miranda about it, and now that she'd read it she did not want to tell her of its existence at all. 'Some things are private,' she said. 'A person's sex life is private.'

'This is not my sex life,' I told her. 'This is nothing to do with my sex life.' I felt alone.

She wanted to throw my words in the bin, she said. She had hoped for a fairy tale ending, but this is no fairy tale, she said. This is devastating. She was frightened of what my words might do.

I was upset to hear her say these things. I was a child too, I found myself wanting to say, and then felt guilty for those feelings. Oh, the cost of all this. It's just so hard, too hard for anyone to comprehend.

Later though, I admired a mother so fiercely protective of her daughter.

'Think before you decide on her behalf,' I said finally. 'Maybe tell her you have the story and give her the choice. She can always say no.'

Some time later, I got an email from her saying that she had passed the story on to Miranda, that she wasn't sure how Miranda had responded but that Miranda was glad her other mother hadn't kept it from her.

Months later I heard from Miranda. Actually, I didn't exactly hear from her. She wrote to her other mother and told her she didn't know how to respond to me. Her mother was pressuring her to respond and she didn't know how to. She was so glad her mother was her mother. Although I said several times in the story that I made the wrong decision, she was sure I made the right decision. She didn't have room for me in her life. She wasn't sure how she felt after reading the story. She couldn't see how she could possibly go forward. Maybe her mother should just copy the email to me, she said. And this is what her other mother did.

Some time later, she wrote to me and said other things; how difficult this was, how confusing. We emailed one another from then on. I don't recall much about the content of the emails. I sent her the names of songs. I don't know if she ever listened to them. 'I Dream a Highway' by Gillian Welch. At least one song by Geoffrey Gurrumul Yunupingu. 'Make You Feel My Love' by Bob Dylan. She told me about her life, her real life.

PART IV

Arriving

Byron swim

TODAY I SWAM THE BAY and didn't feel afraid. I went out through The Pass and the sea was easy, if mildly resistant. Near the rocks, I bumped into a skindiver in a dark grey wetsuit. I took him for a shark. He took me for his diving buddy. When we realised we were neither of us who we thought, we laughed and wished each other well. I said hello to everyone I met, kayakers, swimmers, fish, a turtle.

The thing I love about swimming in the sea is the freedom it gives. The water and I are not so different, our bodies going where they will. The sea and I are one just for a little while. I have heard that drowning is a painful and terrifying death. I imagine it to be so, having known even in small measure what failure of breath feels like. I do not wish to drown, would feel the sea had betrayed me, for its beneficence is so pervasive when I swim that I have learned to take it for granted, for mine.

Near the end of the swim I rolled over onto my back and floated a while, as if I am the kind of person who floats a while. Soon a thousand will follow me in the swim I have just done. It is the day of the Ocean Beach Classic, and already the water is dotted with the orange buoys that will show the swimmers their route. I am glad to avoid the throng. I am a good enough swimmer. I do not wish to improve.

I walked back along the beach after my swim and tears came. They have changed just lately. No teeth chattering, no yelling, but sobbing, heart-sobbing, for all that has been lost. Me, who lost some of her youth; baby Ruth, who was torn from the mother she had a right to; and David and Otis, who lost the life they might have lived.

David who is still here beside me, Otis who has no choice about the mother he has, who continues to love me when I am not the mother I want to be. They are there now, building a castle from the stones we found on the beach on the other side of The Pass. They will be there when I arrive, and they will wave and their wave will say, We are here, we love you. And I will wave back.

Rosemary

MY MOTHER TOOK A HANDBAG everywhere she went. Her final one was a supermarket freezer bag. I don't know what was in her handbag—everything you might need to survive the last days, I suspect. She hardly ever let me carry it for her, even when she was old and sick. It was very heavy.

Her name was Rosemary, which is my name in reverse, or I suppose mine is hers in reverse, but she didn't mention this and I didn't notice until I was in my teens and someone commented. When I asked her, she said that no, she hadn't called me Mary-Rose because she was Rosemary. It had never occurred to her. She just liked the name. And also, she thought Mary-Rose MacColl might be a name for a writer.

She was a writer too, of course. She was a journalist and later in life she wrote poetry and romance novels. I've often wondered what she might have written if she'd had the opportunities I've had in life to write about my own experiences. But she didn't have the opportunities I've had. She just did what she could to make sure I had them.

When I was a child, she was vast. I remember seeing her body in the bath. These days she would be termed morbidly obese, but I didn't think of her as that. It was part of who she was. She was solid, reassuring, soft. As she got sicker in her last year—cancer that started on her beautiful face—she stopped being able to eat as easily and so her bulk dwindled. She clarified, in a way, into the girl she'd been.

It was Mum who had us all taught to swim. I was that girl of ten standing by the pool because of her. The night I won the only swimming race I ever won, against the faster, larger Mary McCluskey who hadn't perfected, as I had, the speed-enhancing tumble-turn, it was Mum who was there to tell me how marvellous I was.

Mum herself had never learned to swim but one day she jumped into the pool and found that watching swimming instructors all those years had taught her too. She swam effortlessly.

In her very last days, cancer caught her up like the hound it is and the cells burned every last skerrick of fat from her body. On the day she died, her face was just like Nana's; the same fine bones had shown themselves.

For a Girl

‿‿

She'd moved to Perth when Andrew my brother went there for work. She went to visit and found the new place suited her. She liked the climate and the blue sandy river. She liked being a long way away from Nana, and she liked being a long way away from me; in my thirties I was bossy, thought I knew what was best for her. I think she might have liked, too, the notion she might be someone else. She might start again.

I flew to Perth to tell her the truth about my teacher and her husband. We were in McDonald's in Fremantle where, she told me, she could get a burger and coffee with an ice-cream for a dollar on her pension card. Otis and David were down on the beach.

'The father of my baby girl,' I said. 'It was my teacher's husband.'

She knew already, she said. 'I've always known.'

I told her all the truth then, what he had done.

My mother had clear light green eyes, reminiscent of those lakes in Canada when the snow first melts. She looked up at me and put her hand on mine and said, 'Oh, Rose, I'm so sorry I didn't do more. I should have.'

It was a healing gesture at a time when I was feeling treacherous about what I'd done to her, lying about my baby's father. I was feeling treacherous about what I'd done to my child. I was feeling as if I'd betrayed my blood, the strong women I came from.

I told her she couldn't have done more; she was the perfect mother for me. And it is the deepest truth I know.

'Have you had any contact with her?' she said after a while.

'She doesn't want to meet,' I said.

'Of course,' she said. 'She might one day.'

This is what mothers are for.

⌒

The day I took her to the hospice for her first and last visit, she didn't take her handbag. She had metastatic bone cancer by then. The nurses who'd been visiting her at home said it would be respite only, that Mum was managing well. She'd be out in a week, they thought. She still had months.

She'd wanted to die at home. Having seen my bossiness for what it was by this time—an attempt to control a world that will not be controlled—I wanted her to have whatever she wanted.

I told her if they tried to keep her at the hospice, I might not be able to get her out again. I knew about powerful institutions.

She nodded.

She didn't take her handbag.

'Your bag, Mum,' I said. She just shook her head. She knew.

Or almost knew. Because when we arrived at the hospice and the doctor came to see her, she told the doctor she hadn't eaten for nineteen months because her mouth was sore and I think some part of her thought they might fix her now. She might enjoy life again.

⟋⟍

When I wrote *In Falling Snow*, I thought she might not live long enough to read it. It was the first novel I'd written since the long journey I'd been on.

In Falling Snow is historical fiction, and to my own surprise I loved researching the history most of all. It tells the story of extraordinary women who created a hospital in an old abbey in France in World War I. There is a child lost; of course there is. But writing about strong women who overcome difficulties became my thing with *In Falling Snow*: the lost heart, in Louise Bogan's words, that I give back to the world. I followed it with *Swimming Home*, about women swimmers. It is a very small lost heart, the one I give back to the world, but it's the lost heart that's got my name on it.

I got my publisher to send Mum the proofs for *In Falling Snow* so that she could read the novel before she died.

She was so sick by then, and drugged. She kept losing her place, she said, falling asleep reading.

But she'd read it all once, she said, and now she was reading it again.

'It's very good,' she said. 'I'm so proud of you.'

Byron goodbye

OUR TIME HERE AT THE farm is over. Otis will wake soon and we'll pack the car and say goodbye cows, goodbye farm, goodbye beach, goodbye sea.

Goodbye, baby Ruth.

I do not much imagine what our life together would have been like. I do not think of you at two and four and seventeen living with me. It is a baby named Ruth I have been grieving, a potential life that never was.

My body knows Otis at every stage of his life, in my belly, on my breast, in my arms, wrapped around my neck and hips, hand in hand. My body was cut from you at birth, became confused, so all I have is a knowing that once I carried your life, your tiny life, and then it was gone.

I'd have made a mess of mothering you at nineteen. We'd have been poor and friendless. I doubt my teacher and her husband would have given much support, although you never know people, as Nana used to say. I'd probably have made new friends. I'm a good maker of friends, I've discovered. My mother would have helped. I'm sure she would have. But it would have been a hard life for you. I'd have had no job, no money and no ongoing support.

I'd have made a mess of mothering you, which is why when my friend Mary tells me that in all the years she spent working with teenage mothers, she only cared for one family in which the baby might have been better off with someone else, it resonates somewhere deep within me. For while I would have been the worst mother to you in so many ways, I was your mother, your best mother, and should have claimed you.

I am sure I did you harm, although I didn't know it at the time, and you have said you do not agree with me that harm was done. We will have to agree to disagree about that. I am responsible for the months we shared my body in which I didn't acknowledge you. I am responsible for leaving you in a hospital nursery for twelve days, cared for by those lunatic midwives with their gripe water and beliefs, leaving you in foster care with some woman who said a newborn baby was unhappy and waved a Bible over her, leaving you those thirty days until your other mother could come and take you in her arms and try to make it better.

I am responsible for giving you away to strangers.

In our big souls, as Stace calls them, did we know what we were doing, Miranda? Did we each come into this life with something to learn? Perhaps we did. I think I am learning to be happy rather than normal. Is that my lesson?

Whatever else will happen, whatever else has happened, you are on the Earth. What happened to us seared that dark and violent beach with fire. You clung to my unwelcoming womb like a limpet on a rock. You emerged from me in a wave of grief that's taken all these years to find its shore. But you are alive. You are this vibrant woman your other mother describes and loves so well, this marvellous woman who makes her way through the world.

I wish you a life as filled with meaning as mine.

April 2016

LATE LAST YEAR, I WENT TO see a young woman named Bonnie Bliss (possibly not her real name) at Stace's suggestion. Stace had a friend with a story like mine who'd gone to see Bonnie Bliss and it had been helpful.

I've learned that sometimes you have to take a breath and dive in. I decided to make an appointment without thinking too much about it.

Bonnie Bliss offers a three-hour one-on-one yoni-mapping session for women. Yoni is another word for vagina and the mapping is what you might imagine it is. The aim of her work is healing, helping women who've experienced trauma in this part of their bodies back to themselves.

Bonnie Bliss lives and works from a cottage on a farm outside Mullumbimby. When I arrived at the session, she explained that she was pursuing a Tantric spiritual path, which seems to me, from what she then said about it, a lot like Buddhism.

I don't know if Bonnie Bliss helps other people, those who haven't experienced what I have, but she helped me.

⌒

Last month, the Royal Commission into Institutional Responses to Child Abuse was in Brisbane, bringing its light to dark places where people who have done great harm have hidden for a very long time. Although it does me no good, I read the testimonies of children, now grown, who were betrayed by those who had a duty to care for them. I read the responses of the schools and institutions, those who run them even worse in their way than the offenders, for they have more resources. They know about harm. They are able to tell the difference between right and wrong.

After I watch the Royal Commission for a week, I do something I haven't done for years. I look up my teacher and her husband by name on the internet. I find a funeral notice. My teacher's husband has died peacefully in his sleep, it says. I am supposed to feel something, I know, but for weeks nothing is there. Nothing at all. I think of going to the cemetery, finding those bricks, burying them, but I realise they are already buried, already gone.

And then I write to the Royal Commission, offer my name, my teacher's name, her husband's, offer to tell my story if it will help anyone else. I get a call from a commission officer, whose job it is to check whether my situation fits the commission's terms of reference.

I was older than many of those who've given evidence, I tell him.

Yes, he says.

The school was not to blame here.

All right, he says.

He wants to know did I ever lodge a formal complaint about what happened.

I did not, I say, wondering if he thinks me daft, writing after all this time.

'Your story is as set out in your letter?' he asks.

Yes.

'The next step is for you to meet with a commissioner,' he says.

It may take up to a year to arrange. They have so many of us to meet with, there's a backlog.

I'll wait, I say.

Home

WE AGREED ON A CAFE in the middle of the Fitzroy Gardens. It was spring or summer, I don't remember, but the day was perfect. I was late—the plane, the bus, a long walk.

We were texting one another like two friends.

Sorry, longer walk than I thought.

The reply: *Don't fret, see you soon.*

So normal.

So normal. But in the approaching days, my body had set out on its own journey. I had passed through menopause in the intervening years, but now I had all the signs of ovulation: an ache on that right side, the coveted egg white, and then that heaviness in my pelvis, as if preparing for new life.

My body remembers. It remembers everything.

Finally, I got through the gardens, the leaves on those lovely elms, the green grass. I saw her standing at the cafe doors and knew her, although I didn't have a recent photograph and hadn't asked for one. When we embraced, when we crossed that enormous space, I felt her slight shoulders and they were shaking. I realised she was nervous.

Oh God, *she* was nervous. I had done wrong to her, my child, and she was nervous. The cost. But more than that, I realised, here was a person, with a sense of humour and a preference for honesty and a winning smile, her own. I realised here was a person and it was enough.

I had read so many stories of mothers reconnecting with their children. I expected it would be of the nature of epiphany. It was not. There was a long rough road ahead, given where we'd started, and no guarantee of anything at all. It was not of the nature of epiphany. But it was of the nature of something good and right in the world. And it was enough for the rest of life.

Writer's note

IF BOOKS WERE SONGS, SINGING this one required a leap
into the mosh pit. My colleagues Karyn Brinkley, Kris Olsson,
Julieanne Schultz and Fiona Stager heard an early tune and
didn't shun me. On the contrary, they encouraged me to
leap into the crowd.

The leaping skills of Stace Callaghan, Shar Edmunds and
Wayne McLeod helped me find the trajectory and courage.
Fiona Inglis was there to catch me; it stays with you when
someone does that. The crowd has included gentle hands,
Lenore Cooper, Cherrell Hirst, Suzi Jefferies, Mary Philip,
Louise Ryan, Cathy Sinclair and Theanne Walters, who lifted
me along, and Ellen and Maddie, who know stuff.

The Banff Centre and Wild Flour Bakery Café in Banff
and Byron Bay Farmstay in northern New South Wales

provided snow or sea and safe places in the maelstrom, as well as folk I've come to love.

My forever band is Allen & Unwin, Christa Munns, who ensures we don't falter musically, not once, Ali Lavau, who co-writes these days, Marg Langvizer, on song since the start, and Annette Barlow, who leads with love and turns songs into hits. She makes us rock stars!

Kim Wilkins, another rock star, listened to every version of this song and understood. Read her *Daughters of the Storm*.

The 103 bus passengers, Georgie, Fin, Otis and Wil, made my mornings sing, and Otis makes every leap of faith rewarded.

David held my hand and jumped without hesitating.

Wasn't I lucky?

Mary-Rose MacColl
14 January 2017